Find Your Soul Path

DISCOVER THE
MAGICAL LIFE WITHIN

EMMA GRIFFIN

DAVID & CHARLES

www.davidandcharles.com

Contents

Introduction

I was raised within a spiritual family, so I have always led a more mystical way of life. My mother was a witch who created fantasy art and did Tarot readings, eventually painting and publishing her own deck. She had an incredible imagination and was always making up the most wonderful stories of make-believe worlds. She regularly brought the spirit world into our daily lives as children – after family meals we would often do seances together and she did Tarot readings for us all. It was normal for me to have this in my life. My mother taught me to believe in magic and the belief that anything is possible.

I can still remember the first time I had a conversation with a spirit, at the age of four. My mother never said it was wrong, or that spirits didn't exist, so it was a very natural journey for me to carry on working with the spirit world.

My father worked in the fashion industry and had a passion for travel and culture, as well as an interest in spirituality, and loved to attend the large spiritual fairs in London each year. He was also a medium who performed at local pubs and spiritual church events. He taught me how to meditate and the importance of that practice. He also explained to me about our own human energy frequency and the different dimensions, which has always fascinated me.

At the age of twenty – and at the start of my full spiritual awakening – I was divinely guided to learn everything I could about the afterlife and understand the meaning behind spirituality. As I began to reconnect with my intuition, I experienced a series of encounters with mediums, psychics, shamans, energy healers and wise women that further expanded my awareness. These new relationships led me to discover my own healing abilities and deeper connection to the spirit world, while also becoming increasingly sensitive to the energy of those around me. This also led me to becoming a witch.

When I discovered witchcraft, it really felt like I was returning home. It felt so natural to me. I started this path as a Wiccan Witch and over the years this guided me to a more relaxed eclectic path with my craft. From the day I stepped into witchcraft, I have used it every day for over twenty-five years.

During my life, I have had to overcome many difficulties, which have taught me so much about life and about myself. When I had just entered my thirties I became ill with cancer and my outcome didn't look great. My mother was reading a book called *The Secret* that was having a profound effect on her life and suggested I should study it as it might really help me in my situation.

The Secret is about the Law of Attraction – what you think about, you attract. The one thing that didn't sit well with me was the term "think positive all the time". Now, you can't think positive thoughts all the time! You can't beat yourself and think, "Oh no, I don't feel positive, so now my manifestations won't work!" So, it sparked something in me to reflect on in my whole life. What have I struggled with, where there was trauma or pain, and how I have manifested up to this point.

I realized that my knowledge of witchcraft mixed with my spiritual beliefs really had become the anchor in my life and gave me faith. I understood for the first time that I held the power within me to change the situation with my health. After a decade, I was cancer-free, and I truly believe that I have manifested that, supported by my family and excellent medical treatment.

In 2019, I sadly lost my father to cancer and within a few months of his passing, my mother also became ill with cancer. My life turned upside down and I felt truly lost, which led me to another great spiritual awakening.

At this point in my life, I had built my own successful photography business, and I decided to dedicate some of my down time to creating a space and environment that could help my mother through her various cancer treatments; a space where I could give her Reiki healing and a place for her to relax. I rented a small studio, decorating it with dried flowers and lovely fabrics so it was comfortable for her. This studio was called The Sacred Space. Over time, I allowed other women in need to come for healing and to hold space for them whilst still dividing my time with being a photographer.

My mother taught me to believe in magic and the belief that anything is possible.

Ways To Find Your Soul Path

Over the years, I have become aware that to live a more present heart-centred life, there are rules that I live by naturally, and there are values and beliefs that really anchor me into this way of living.

1. Living your life to your fullest potential can only be achieved when you have come face-to-face with your fear of the unknown.

2. To be able to conquer your fear of the unknown, you have to be committed to making the changes within yourself.

3. Every action generates a force of energy that returns to us. Choosing actions that bring happiness and success for others ensures the flow of happiness and success to you.

4. Seek your purpose. Discover your unique gifts. Ask yourself how you are best suited to serve humanity. Using your unique gifts and serving others brings unlimited bliss and abundance.

5. Take time to be silent, to just BE. Meditate for 30 minutes twice a day. Silently witness the beauty within every living thing. THIS is the biggest medicine in life.

6. To manifest your desires, you must match your vibration with that of what you want.

7. Be happy in this present time, in this present moment.

8. Protect your own vibration. Set boundaries and surround yourself with people that help make you shine.

9. You must have some kind of vision for your life. Even if you do not know the plan, you have a direction in which you choose to go.

10. If you want to be happy, you have to love YOURSELF!

In September 2020, my mother passed away in my arms at home. The grief and heartbreak re-opened me to something which had been calling me my entire life. I began to meditate every day as it served as the best medicine to help me through that time. Losing both of your parents so close to each other really is something I can't put into words.

Finally, I surrendered to the path the Universe was guiding me towards and quit my full-time job as an editorial photographer and jumped fully into The Sacred Space as a witch, a channeller and mystical mentor. My intention was to guide women to intuitively heal their emotions by learning how to connect to their heart space, to listen to and navigate their emotions from the soul; to connect with their body, their own energy field, to receive guidance, discern fear from intuition and use the power of intention to manifest their dream life; guiding others to reconnect to their inner wisdom and to make peace with the past.

A few years have now passed, which has allowed me a considerable amount of time for inner reflection. Throughout my own journey I was forever searching for that feeling of truly being at home. It was only when I took the first step to connect back to myself, listening to that voice within and learning to love myself, did I find happiness. Over time, I realized that the feeling I was

searching for wasn't from a person or a place. I had spent all that time searching only to realize that it had been inside me all along, it is within that present moment when I am connecting to my heart.

When we have unpacked our past, our fears and the things that hold us back, we can support ourselves with our daily practices and put into place small rituals that align us to our soul path within the container of our home. This is what this book is all about – to get you onto this path, and everything you need to place you back into alignment with your own soul path.

Who is this book for?

I use the term woman and women throughout the book but this extends to all female-identifying and non-binary beings. Writing this book is how I can share with others everything that I have learnt to live a soul-based life. I want your lives to transform as mine did. Within this book I share tools, practices and techniques to help you fall madly in love with your true self, to connect to your authentic self and create the life you've been dreaming about – with the added help of a little magic!

Sacred Home

Sacred Spaces within the home are a huge part of my spiritual practice, as a highly visual and creative person what I see around me significantly affects my wellbeing. I've been actively creating Sacred Spaces my entire life.

I have a background in interior design, so I have seen first-hand how a beautiful environment in a home influences that homeowner's energy. In my own home, I frequently move the rooms around, re-decorate and play with the styling. Part of this is because of my sensitivity to energy – by moving things it changes the energy around me. We all do this to some degree, for example when you invite people over, you clean and tidy up, maybe also lighting candles or incense. Creating a Sacred Space is a ritual in itself – making a magical space to spend quality time full of intention.

After having my first child, I had lots of down time in between feeding and playing. I felt drawn to a certain part of the home that had a calming feeling and I could rest. Gradually, that space became sacred to me, I looked forward to that time to reboot and have time for myself. Now my two children are adults and there is a little more space in the house, that one small area that I returned to became a whole room dedicated as my own Sacred Space. I surrounded myself with meaningful items that light up my soul and make my heart sing, and created a dedicated altar. This is my space where I sit and meditate, pull cards, journal and connect to spirits.

Over the years, this one dedicated space became the whole house. It's so important to me to have little areas within our house that make me feel a sense of returning home, spaces in which to be fully present and connect to my inner self. My soul NEEDS to have these sacred areas throughout our home – spaces that relax me or lift me up.

The saying "home is where the heart is" can be interpreted as home is wherever our loved ones are, and I genuinely feel it's at home that our hearts are filled with happiness and love. The home is our container of happiness. It nurtures our wellness and to me it is the most important first step of putting ourselves back into alignment with our soul path. Your home is an extension of personal energy. This is why when you clean, rearrange furniture and get rid of objects that are cluttering your space it has such a profound impact on your mind, body and spirit.

Home is Where the Heart is

Creating a Sacred Space

Today our home now mirrors back to me my authentic self, it keeps me in touch with my true self-worth. I have noticed how this has affected my whole family living in our home and the people who come to visit. Everyone instantly feels at peace, they enjoy looking around at all of the treasures. By creating this Sacred Space in our home, it is constantly giving great energy to everyone who enters it.

Personal tastes differ massively. What I find to be stimulating or relaxing might not be the same for you. Personally, I love to create magical, light, fresh spaces, inspired by an earthy, rustic and bohemian style. I am a huge Harry Potter fan, so I love to have magical items around me that are also a reminder to always be childlike, have fun and remind me of my mother's guidance of believing in magic.

I am drawn to calming colours that are inspired by nature, I love wood, cosy textures and, of course, lots of plants. As a creative, I also like to be surrounded by art and antiques, special finds that hold so much history within them. Our home has become a beautiful container of relaxation, every last corner of each room fills me with joy every time I enter.

Scents are as crucial to styling a room and your home as the visual element. This could literally be as simple as lighting a favourite candle. You can also burn dried ethically sourced plants. Sage, for example, is often associated with purification, which is therefore perfect for when you move into a new space. Mugwort welcomes psychic dreams, while sweetgrass calls on your ancestors' energy and invites positive spirits into the space.

Personally, I love any incense that has a predominant rose scent. The rose is such a powerful flower that holds unconditional love within its energy, ideal to burn in a family home. I also use lavender essential oils in my oil burner, which radiates such a calming energy. If I want to feel re-energized, I usually opt for pine. Smell is a powerful sense and is incredible for influencing brain activity, so why not use it in your home more consciously.

Here are a few of my favourite scents to help create a happy home environment.

- **Lavender** – has calming properties and has a soothing effect on nerves, it can relieve nervous tension as well as treat headaches and migraines.

- **Jasmine** – can also be used to calm nerves. This oil is commonly used as an antidepressant because of its uplifting energy.

- **Lemon** – great for when you are feeling run down. Lemon boosts the body's immune system and is wonderful for improving circulation.

- **Rosemary** – is my go-to pick-me-up smell. Rosemary has stimulating properties that help with mental fatigue. It is also calming and will improve memory retention.

- **Peppermint** – is the real energy booster, this scent wakes up the mind and stimulates clear thinking.

- **Rose** – brings a renewed sense of balance and calm.

- **Pine** – is perfect after a hectic day as it will decrease anxiety, and lower depression and stress levels.

Inside Space

For me, the lounge is the heart of our home. This room holds us, and we relax at the end of the day, but it is also where our family and friends join together. Located in an integral position within this space is my coffee table, which has taken on the form of another altar. I have gathered candles, nature, crystals and small carved items found in an antiques shop that have become especially meaningful to me. My preference in the evenings is to use candlelight or fairy lights rather than overhead ceiling lights. My feeling is that strong electric lighting disconnects us from nature and the Universe.

The bedroom is probably the most important room within your home and should be a relaxing environment. This space informs how we rest and recover, how we fall asleep and how we wake.

When it came to styling our bedroom, I made notes on how I wanted that room to hold space for me – I considered how I use that space and what energy I needed from it. I am very fortunate to be able to work from home, so I do not have to be up and on it first thing every day! I love to wake a little earlier so that I can have time for slow mornings; sitting in bed while I drink my first coffee of the day, gazing out of the window to the garden is a beautiful way to start my day. Reflecting on this, I decided to bring the outside into the room by using the colour green.

As previously mentioned, I am all about surrounding myself with items that bring me joy, so art, candles, crystals, plants and objects that make me smile or trigger a happy memory have been introduced. Textures and comfort have a massive role in the bedroom – I love a nice quality duvet set, cushions and throws.

Colours for your bedroom that will help bring in calm are:

- **Green** – represents nature and peace.
- **Yellow** – represents energy and happiness.
- **Orange** – represents security and stability. Its calming influence makes it a brilliant colour choice for bedrooms.
- **Pink** – represents heat and passion. Soft baby pink is more calming, but overall pink represents love.
- **Brown** – represents the earth, nature, stability and can create a very calm, serene room.

Dining Space

One of my other favourite areas of the home is our family table, the dining space. Setting a table is a ritual in itself. When a table is set with intention it becomes more memorable. The setting of a table connects back to gathering, sharing, talking, eating and healing together as a family.

I love to set the table for my family and my friends, especially for a sabbat holiday, because I can add themes to the setting and always bring in nature. I also love to set a table outside to eat under the stars in the summer months, connecting to nature and using natural treasures as decoration.

When you place intention into doing this, you will see the energy rise for your guests. They will notice and be influenced by this energy, which will bring them joy. To me, it is an extension of love: being intentional in creating this beautiful table, gathering together, talking and sharing good food is one of our greatest gifts. It can be inspiring, uplifting, and I believe we as a collective should be slowing down more and enjoying simple life moments like these.

When it comes to buying items for our home and for table settings, I love to buy second-hand items or unique pieces made by local designers. By creating a more sacred home it will also make you more conscious when you buy new items, such as mugs, decorations, fabrics, etc. The aim here is to buy only what fires up your heart, so that when you see or feel the items it lifts up your soul.

Your home is your Sacred Space, which is your container of your wellness, a container to hold space for your personal growth.

Outside Space

Equally important to your home is the garden or outside space that can improve your wellbeing in so many ways. The main way it does this is by helping us feel calmer and more centred. For example, when you have a busy stressful life, being in your garden, planting and nurturing your plants helps to refocus the mind, elevating us away from the stresses of our everyday lives.

I am lucky to have a few special magical spaces within my garden. One of my favourite spots is down towards the bottom where I have two witchy sheds and a swing bench that is in the shade of a hazel tree. I'm not particularly a sun lover and am quite pale so I need to be in cool shaded areas where I can sit and reflect. During the magic hour, as the sun slowly sets, is my favourite time to wander down, taking my journal, a nice drink and reflecting on my day. It's so peaceful.

Again, it's all about the smells, textures and light for me. My soul responds well to these and it becomes a container of wellness to support my reflection time.

There are several things that you might like to incorporate into your garden or outside space, everyone will have a unique take on what helps us bring our own sense of peace.

- The first thing to anchor into is what will bring you joy to look at?

- What will bring you peace?

- Do you prefer shade, would you rather be in the sun, or a mix of both?

- Do you want it to feel intimate and enclosed?

- Or would you prefer expansive views?

You could be creative and divide the space in your garden allowing you to create separate areas, such as one for dining and one for relaxing.

Personally, I have allowed my favourite magical area to be more wild with the focus on greenery as it's naturally relaxing to the eye. I have a focus point in the form of a pentagram, which helps me to be anchored into my inner personal power. There is also a lovely old wheelbarrow that is filled with wild flowers and rosemary.

There is nothing I like more than sitting and relaxing, smelling frankincense resin burning in a cauldron while I close my eyes and drift off into a daydream.

Crystals

Being an empath and working with energy, crystals are a big part of my life. Growing up, my mother always placed different-sized crystals in all of the rooms and showed us how we could connect with them. Naturally, this is mirrored in my adult life. Crystals are all around our home in every single room, used to radiate out different energy frequencies. The best crystal is ultimately whichever one speaks to you. I encourage people to touch base with what they are drawn to and what feels good when they hold it.

Crystals for the bedroom: rose quartz and amethyst. I like to partner these two together on our nightstand. This energy combination brings perfect balance. Rose quartz connects with the heart chakra to open the soul up to love with another but also for rediscovering self-love. It holds a soft energy that is great to soothe the remaining tensions from the day. Amethyst is a natural healer, brings comfort and can also help you to recall your dreams.

Crystals for the living room: amethyst and fluorite. A natural healer and stress reliever, amethyst is ideal for a relaxing space. It clears negativity and radiates out positive energy. It's one of those crystals for the home that you can't go wrong placing in any room of the house! Fluorite will bring balance and harmony to the room, and will cultivate positivity that is perfect for a relaxing night in.

Crystals for the bathroom: clear quartz and rose quartz. Clear quartz is great for the bathroom. Have it by the shower or bath to enhance the energy of cleansing. Clear quartz is an amplifier, and works to magnify the energy of your spirit. It will purify your spirit at the same time as you cleanse your body. Rose quartz, with its gentle energy, will help you to relax when you're washing away the stress of the day. Having a rose quartz in the bathroom will remind you to indulge in self-care.

Here's a beginner's guide to which crystal you can use in order to harness the energy you're seeking.

- **Amethyst:** calming and intuition.
- **Onyx:** protection, absorbs and transforms negative energy.
- **Pyrite:** protection, shields from negative energy.
- **Clear Quartz:** clarity in thinking, improved awareness and memory.
- **Rose Quartz:** forgiveness, peace and compassion.
- **Tiger Eye:** confidence, strength, courage and good luck.
- **Selenite:** clarity of mind, anti-anxiety, soothing, concentration.
- **Moonstone:** new beginnings, intuition, enhancement of psychic abilities.
- **Hematite:** energy and vitality.
- **Jade:** emotional balance, peace, purity.
- **Aquamarine:** soothes fears, reduces stress and quietens the mind.
- **Obsidian:** deep psychic cleanse, protection against negative energies.

Altars

An altar is a Sacred Space where you can place all your favourite, meaningful, spiritual and mystical items, and where you can come back to for healing, inspiration, meditation, spiritual rituals or spell work. Engaging with my altar as part of my daily practice gives me something to regularly lean into even when life is difficult.

Altars can be as simple or as elaborate as you want – it's entirely up to you. I would like to inspire and encourage you to have two altars in your own Sacred Space.

1. The first would be your main altar – this could be a shelf or top of a unit so you can always see it.

2. The second is a floor altar – a space where you sit and meditate. Mine is such a special and integral part of my practice as it always feels so sacred to me. You will need a small space where you can sit on a cushion in meditation and have enough room for this small altar in front of you, again adding items that fire you up.

MAIN ALTAR

This symbolizes your innermost self and spirituality. It is a representation of your hopes, your wishes, the things you're working on or releasing. A place to set intentions and to light up your manifestations. Altars are also focal points for your practice. It is a place to get back in touch with your authentic self. The more you spend time at your altar space, the more peaceful energy will be infused there.

Here are some things to consider when creating your home altar. Remember the following are all just suggestions from my years of working with these spaces. In the end, there are no rules – your altar can look like anything and be placed anywhere as long as it makes you happy.

Here's a list of things your altars would usually incorporate:

- Photos of your ancestors.
- Crystals.
- Candles.
- Written affirmations.
- Flowers and herbs.
- Statues.
- Pictures or objects that remind you of what you're manifesting.
- A journal.
- Tarot or oracle cards.
- Incense.

THE SUN

APRIL

JULY

OCTOBER

CACTI · SUCCULENTS

If you're using different flowers and herbs on your altar, here's a guide for what you can use to harness different energies.

- **Thyme:** for activation.
- **Acorns:** for never-ending life.
- **Sage:** for cleansing and promotes good health.
- **Roses:** for love.
- **Cinnamon:** for healing, cleansing and used in psychic work.
- **Heather:** for protection and for granting wishes.
- **Lavender:** for healing and peace.
- **Basil:** for letting go of what is no longer needed.
- **Jasmine:** for kindness and romance.
- **Oak leaves:** for protection, power and strength.

You may want to incorporate the elements, so consider the following:

- **Fire:** a candle.
- **Air:** a feather.
- **Water:** a shell or jar of rainwater.
- **Earth:** a plant, a rock or even a small bowl of soil.

Deciding where to set up your altar is an intuitive process. You need to pick a space where you feel present and spiritually connected. It can be a table, a windowsill, an area outside in a garden or a corner in your home.

Regularly give your altar some care, which will become a ritual of its own. Think about dusting and organizing it every week, removing wilted flowers for fresh ones, and adding new offerings that reflect your current intentions.

For my floor altar, I use a pouffe and place a cauldron in the middle, which I use to burn incense for letting go of what no longer serves me (in a fire ritual). I place the crystals I use while in my morning routine, a white candle and my oracle deck so I am all ready to start my daily practice.

All the ideas for your main altar can be applied to a floor altar and can be changed daily to whatever energy you are of in need.

There are no limits to what crystals or other sacred objects you place on your altar. The design and objects are entirely up to you to create your most optimal Sacred Space.

Cleansing Your Sacred Space

Once you have created your Sacred Space, it is important to bless and cleanse it. Using smoke is one of the ways to energetically cleanse a space to invite positive energy. When doing this, you burn dried plant material, the smoke then fills and cleanses the environment.

Smudge sticks are derived from Native American culture, where they are used in ceremonies to cleanse and bless people and places. The sticks are usually made up of dried sage, but can be made with whatever combinations of dried herbs and flowers you prefer.

Since the purpose of smoke cleansing is to cleanse and freshen a space, choose herbs that you love the smell of.

HOW TO MAKE A SMOKE WAND

1. Gather the ingredients you wish to work with. For a basic smoke wand, I use rosemary and fresh sage from our garden.

2. Layer your herbs, positioning the largest leaves at the same level as one another, holding them tightly in your hand.

3. Cut a piece of cotton string and make a simple loose knot at one end of the string. Wrap the cotton around the bundle, from the bottom to the top.

Bundles You Can Burn

★ Rosemary

★ Lavender

★ Mugwort

★ Cinnamon sticks

Cleansing like this is an ancient ceremony in which sacred plants are burned, and the resulting smoke is wafted throughout a space or around someone's body. How often do you need to smoke cleanse? I do this when I am feeling stuck, negative or sluggish. Feeling like this may be due to some bad energy in your aura. I would recommend clearing your energy once a week and your space/home once a month.

Every full moon I smoke cleanse our whole home. I start at the front door moving clockwise around the house. Then I return to the centre of the home, which is our lounge and say:

Smoke Of Air

Fire And Earth

Cleanse And Bless

This Home

Drive Away

All Harm And Fear

Only Good

May Enter Here.

4. Once you reach the top of the bundle, go back on yourself, down to the start. Continue wrapping and crisscrossing the string as you get towards the base of the bundle. Remember to pull tight as you bind the bundle together (the herbs will shrink slightly once dried). Tie the loose end to the original knot at the base of the wand.

5. Hang your smoke wand upside down in a sunny spot to dry for about three weeks.

HOW TO USE A SMOKE WAND

Light one end of your smoke wand with a match, allow it to start burning and then blow out the flame. You can fan the smoke with a feather or your hand. It's helpful to hold a bowl or shell underneath to catch any burning embers. It may go out a lot, so don't worry if you have to relight it. You can also place the wand in a fire-proof bowl or shell while the wand is burning.

You can cleanse yourself or your home whenever you feel you need to. There is no right or wrong way. When I cleanse myself, I start at the top of my head and move down my body even under my feet.

When I am cleansing our home, I start at our front door wafting the smoke clockwise and then I move around each room in our home in a clockwise direction. When you move around your room or home it is good to hold an intention in your mind while you are cleansing. As you walk around, visualize the old, stagnant energy dissolving and fresh energy taking its place.

When you are finished, you can place the smoke wand in a fire-proof bowl away from anything flammable and allow it to slowly burn itself out or run it under cold water and allow the herbs to dry out again.

I also really like to use frankincense resin a lot as I LOVE how it makes me feel. Frankincense is a natural sap from trees and used for many things such as:

• Helping with meditation.

• Lifting your mood.

• Clearing your space from negativity.

• Helping promote a good night's sleep.

To use this resin, you need a disc of charcoal and a heatproof dish. Carefully light the charcoal disc by holding it with tweezers into the flame of a candle. The charcoal will crackle and slightly spark. Place it into a heatproof dish then add the resin onto the disc. It will produce a wonderful smelling smoke. As the smoke ascends, your desires and intentions rise and combine into the Universe.

SIMMER POTS

Another way I cleanse or change the energy in our home is by creating a simmer pot, which is a pan of water filled with herbs, fruits or flowers that while heating on your stove creates a beautiful fragrance in your home. This can be so uplifting.

Here is my favourite Cleansing Simmer:

- ½ cup salt
- 1 teaspoon whole cloves
- ½ cup dried chamomile
- 2 to 3 drops peppermint oil
- The peel and juice of two lemons
- 5 cinnamon sticks

Place two cups of water into your saucepan. While the water is heating up, mix the simmer ingredients in a bowl using your hands. Focus on what your intent is. Pour the herbs into the water and let it simmer on a low heat. Stir occasionally clockwise to bring things towards you and anticlockwise to get rid of things. While it simmers, you will need to add more water so that the ingredients do not burn.

HOUSE SPELL

As well as using sacred smoke, I like to work with rosemary and water collected at a full moon to wash away the old and bring in the new. You can also add the moon water to a bowl on your altar. Add in the rosemary and place a lit white tea light candle to float in it. Focus on your intent of removing stagnant energy and bring in new abundant energy.

Here is a simple spell to help keep negative energy from getting into your house.

You will need:

- 3 cloves of garlic
- Handful of salt
- Handful of rosemary
- Pestle and mortar

Grind and stir everything together in your pestle and mortar. On a full moon leave this mixture in a bowl on a windowsill. The next day, take the mixture outside and spread it along your windowsills on the ground floor and draw a line of the mixture across your doorway. This is the line where your door opens to your home, so usually under your door mat.

If you feel there is low vibrational energy in your home and you don't want to use smoke, you can charge a black crystal like tourmaline, obsidian or onyx to absorb any negativity and protect you. Just hold the stone in your non-dominant hand and then breathe into your heart space, imagining a glowing gold orb growing until it encompasses your whole body, including the stone. Place into your stone your intention by asking it what you want it to do. Then place this stone at the front door of your space, under an entrance mat, on a table or near the back door.

Spiritual Practice

Spiritual practices disconnect us from our minds and help us to realign with our heart space. They help re-ground us when our minds have worked themselves up into a flurry of emotions. I define spiritual practice as something you do every single day that draws you deeper into who you really are by connecting you with your soul. This has a positive impact on our mental health and healing.

My personal spiritual practice guides me back to my soul, brings happiness into my life and helps me to feel centred. Your happiness is a product of your life, your lifestyle, your habits and your daily rituals. If you want to feel and be HAPPY then you must commit yourself to creating that emotion for yourself. My recipe for making my own happiness is laughter with my family, sunshine, fur babies, being in nature, inspiring people and gratitude, all of which make me happy.

To live a Sacred Life, I find the biggest medicine I can give myself is to have a daily spiritual practice. Firstly, you have to accept that practice is essential and then designate the time for it in your daily life. Many people find it easier to maintain regular practice first thing in the morning but this is up to you and your lifestyle.

There are many ways and tools to aid you with spiritual practice. The intention underpinning mine is to calm my mind and body down, connect to my soul, hear my intuition, receive guidance from my ancestors, spirit guides and the Universe.

Everything in the Universe is made up of energy that all vibrates at different frequencies. We all radiate a vibrational frequency; the higher your vibration, the happier you feel, and we can tune into different frequencies.

I personally work with a range of vibrations that I tap into daily:

1. My soul – which is a whisper.

2. My spirit guide – direction and guidance.

3. My loved ones in the spirit world – love.

4. General spirits in the spirit world – chit chat.

5. The Universe – downloads from the source in the form of ideas and direction.

We all have these frequencies to work with, it just takes practice and faith in order to do so. It is through having a spiritual practice that we can work with these frequencies and calm our own mind, body and spirit.

Morning Routine

Mornings can be stressful or busy, so finding a few minutes to start your day with a magical morning routine can make all the difference!

The benefits of a morning routine are:

- Prepare your mind and body for the day in front of you.

- Lower stress and anxiety.

- Enable your ability to focus and be productive.

- Improve energy levels.

- Gain confidence.

- Elevate mood.

- Increase connection to your spiritual self.

- Gain insight into your true self.

- Provide a sense of control for the day.

- Helps to encourage healthy habits.

Morning rituals are all about waking up, setting intentions and preparing yourself for a new day. You can do this even when you make yourself the first hot drink. While you make your morning coffee, try to be present with each step of the process. Imagine putting the energy of love, gratitude, inspiration, motivation or peace into your actions. Notice how it feels as you hold the cup and sip from it. Where do your thoughts go?

Begin to think about your intentions. How would you like them to show up in your day? What would you like to create today? What would you like to experience? What inspires you? What makes you come alive?

Exercise is important. If you have the time, get in a quick bit of exercise, even just 15 minutes of movement can really help shift your energy.

Starting your day with a meditation can be extremely beneficial for balancing and centring yourself for the day ahead. Meditating in the morning also encourages relaxation, mental clarity and focus, which can lead to a more productive day.

Spend a few minutes journaling. Journaling is an incredible way to release negativity and ease a stressful mind. It can also help to focus your energies and thoughts towards what you wish to accomplish during the day. See the Journaling section later in this chapter for more information.

Get empowered while you are getting ready. Pick an outfit that will empower you so you can radiate that positive energy from within. While you are doing your hair or putting on make-up, try to focus your thoughts and visualize how you want to see yourself: confident, beautiful, empowered, happy. If you start to empower yourself and love yourself, others will too.

One of the greatest things you can do for yourself is to show up consistently for your own spiritual practice. Consistency is such a powerful tool, the more you show up to your daily practice, the more connected you will feel. Deciding to show up to a daily practice has been the best decision I've ever made. Show up regularly and you will be surprised how much your life will change for the better. I believe it is so important to check in with your feelings and receive guidance from within.

Pick things that YOU want to do that would really help you start each day in a positive and empowered way. These should be personal and only be those which truly resonate with you.

My morning practice is something I get asked about all the time. When I wake up, I have a cup of coffee sat in bed for about ten minutes. That first drink of coffee is a really relaxing moment. As I sip, I think about what I would like to accomplish in my day. I'm taking just a couple of minutes of quiet, uninterrupted time to focus on these intentions.

Then I get straight onto my running machine. I walk at a good pace whilst listening to an inspiring podcast for 30 minutes. This gives me some extra time to learn whilst also moving my body.

I then get washed, dressed and go downstairs to make myself a mug of sacred cacao. I pour the drink into my favourite mug and head to my Sacred Space. Grabbing my journal and a pen, I then light a white candle, cleanse my room with sacred smoke, place my favourite crystals near me and sit down with my headphones on. I listen to music that doesn't have any words, which really helps me escape my thoughts.

Connecting to my breath and looking into the flame of the candle, I clear my mental and spiritual body, releasing anything that doesn't need to be there now. I then do some breath work, breathing in gratitude, taking a moment to fill my heart space with an intention and then blowing this into my mug of sacred cacao. I then take a sip.

The art of ceremony lies in the power of your intention. When we become fully present, it helps to release limitations and remove blocks from all aspects of our being, helping us to feel, remember and embrace the light we are made of.

At the end of this ceremony, I journal my thoughts. I ask myself things like what does my soul need today?' or 'what messages are there for me to learn?'

Afterwards, I sit for around five to ten minutes and meditate. I actually think I could be one of those people who are addicted to meditation, it really is good for your soul on so many levels. For me, it's a way to connect to my spirit guide, see my ancestors and to go on a journey.

Meditation

Meditation has quite literally changed my life, not only because it's one of the main key tools in manifesting, but it also quietens negative internal voices, fears and emotions. It also relaxes your body so that you can focus on the positive voices, emotions and thoughts that will lead to your success. In my experience, it guides me to my heart space, to feel and hear my soul connecting me with my intuition.

There is so much more to meditation than just relaxing your mind. It can shift your reality and transform your life. Starting the day with meditation slows the mind, helping us to concentrate and focus our early morning thoughts, which in turn helps us to stay in the present moment. It keeps us aware and alert, which will then significantly heighten the quality of our day ahead. Whatever we think about when we first wake up will set the tone for the rest of the day. We can also use this time to let go of any worries or negative thoughts, and this prevents us from beginning the day with mild anxieties.

I then fully journal any insights that have come up for me during my meditation. I pull an oracle card for the day and write about how that resonates with me. I also like to journal my daily experiences and synchronicities to keep track of the magic.

After this process I am then ready to begin my day ahead. AND I feel incredible!

During meditation, you are able to tap into higher vibrational frequencies that will ultimately help you to make the best decisions for yourself. This energy is divine and will always lead you on the path of your highest potential.

When you meditate you can more easily connect to a higher power. It's far simpler and quicker to access this information in a relaxed state, considerably more so than in your everyday waking mind. This divine information will guide you along your path because it knows your soul's true path and ultimately its destination.

Meditating is my most valued practice and it's my biggest form of my own self-care. Meditation is so important – when you pay attention to your breath, you are learning how to return to the present moment. It is so beneficial to your wellness and overall health. Meditation is known to enhance the flow of constructive thoughts and positive emotions. Even a few minutes spent meditating regularly can make a big difference.

Meditation is powerful for getting you into the state to create your own reality and receive divine guidance, which will ultimately lead you on the right path towards your goals.

A BASIC MEDITATION

Take a seat on a large cushion on the floor, sit on the bed or lie down, whatever you find most comfortable. You can sit in a chair with your feet on the floor, you can sit loosely cross-legged, you can kneel – all are fine. Just make sure you are stable and in a position you can stay in for a while.

Choose a place that feels calm and quiet to you.

Set a time limit. If you're just beginning, it can help to choose a short time, for example five or 10 minutes.

Notice your body.

Feel your breath.

Follow the sensation of your breath as it goes in and as it goes out.

Notice when your mind has wandered. Inevitably, your attention will leave the breath and wander to other places. When you get around to noticing that your mind has wandered – in a few seconds, a minute, five minutes – simply return your attention to the breath.

Be kind to your wandering mind. Don't judge yourself or obsess over the content of the thoughts you find yourself lost in. Just come back.

When you're ready, open your eyes. Take a moment and notice any sounds in the environment. Notice how your body feels right now. Notice your thoughts and emotions.

Then journal:

1. What happened?

2. How long was it before your mind wandered away from your breath?

3. Did you notice how busy your mind was even without consciously directing it to think about anything in particular?

4. Did you notice yourself getting caught up in thoughts before you came back to reading this?

When you master meditation for a long period of time you will begin to experience visions while you're meditating. I call this an astral meditation or a spiritual meditation. The visions that you see might be of your current spirit guide, or could directly be a message from your soul. The images you see will have the sensation that somehow they are important for you to pay attention to.

The greatest benefit of spiritual meditation is the pure sense of bliss. You feel so confident in the fact that you are doing exactly what you're supposed to be doing in life.

This kind of meditation is a highly individual experience. I personally find myself passing through dimensions, then connecting to my guides and ancestors. I receive guidance and messages that fire up my heart in so many ways, and it has become a very important part of my daily practice and general wellbeing.

When you meditate in this way you can feel like you're one with everything around you and even as though you are part of the entire Universe. It's a deeply spiritual experience that combines a sense of oneness with the Universe, nature and all living things. During these meditations, you might find that you have no awareness of time, almost like time itself has stopped and you're in a state of timelessness. This can be extremely helpful if you're struggling with anxiety.

I recommend keeping a meditation journal to record visions, images, words or songs you may receive, as this will help you to better articulate what your soul is trying to express.

Journaling

Journaling is a simple practice that will improve mental clarity, offer the ability to see the big picture of our lives, and serve as a catalogue of every success we've ever had.

It's impossible not to spiritually grow when it comes to journal writing. Through the process of writing about your thoughts and feelings, you are decluttering your mind and making it easier for the brain to process.

Here are some of the ways I use journaling in my daily life:

Morning: Firstly, I will write a few sentences relating to my dreams. After my daily meditation, I'll take a few minutes to note everything I experienced during my meditation, any messages or clarity I received.

Throughout my day: I'm incredibly intuitive and get many messages daily. They are often giving me guidance on what to do next. I always write these down so that I can refer back to them when I need to.

When I feel stressed or full of fears: When I am feeling fear, I instantly stop what I am doing, I light a white candle in front of me and pull out my pen and journal. Connecting to my breath to still my thoughts, I begin to write down what I am fearful of. I then close my eyes, connect to my breath and heart space and I ask my SOUL the same question, what am I fearful of? Those two answers are usually very different – one comes from the mind space, the other comes from the heart space. My heart is where the soul is and my mind is where the limited beliefs come from that are linked to the programming I have picked up along the way. By stopping the feelings of fear and directing them in my journal in this way, I always FEEL what action is needed to stop the anxiety.

Manifestations: I jot them all down into my journal, crafting lists of what I want to call into my life, which I can keep and refer back to. For cleansing and letting go, I write down what I am letting go of, then rip this page out and burn it under the full moon.

Gratitude: I finish every journal entry by listing a minimum of three things that I am grateful for from that day. This is a lovely way to attract more positivity and abundance into your life.

SOME JOURNAL PROMPTS FOR YOU TO WORK WITH

★ *When did you feel the happiest in life? Why?*

★ *What was your favourite hobby as a child? Do you still enjoy it?*

★ *When's the last time you showed yourself deep self-care?*

★ *Which everyday habits make you feel the best? List at least ten.*

★ *What are your current goals for personal growth? How are you working towards them?*

★ *What are your current career goals? How are you working towards them?*

★ *What are your current life goals? How are you working towards them?*

★ *What drives you? What do you feel passionate about?*

★ *If you continued life as you are right now, where would you be in five years? Are you happy with that?*

★ *How can you improve your mental health?*

Cacao

I've previously mentioned cacao as part of my morning ritual, so what is it and how do I work with it? The sacred cacao helps us to open our hearts, allowing the body to tap into deeper states of emotional and spiritual knowledge and let go of stress and anxiety. Some of the benefits of cacao are:

- It increases blood flow to our brain.

- Its perfect ratio of calcium and magnesium helps us relax.

- Creates bliss and joy chemicals.

- Heart opening and healing effects.

- Enhances meditation, peace and clarity.

- Promotes creativity.

My own sacred cacao practice is where I sit in total stillness until my thoughts settle. It's here I feel the truth of my heart. The sacred cacao helps me to feel my heart, and its energy moves to the mind as I surrender into the now.

I personally find it so important that we do things that help us take care of our mental, physical and spiritual health. A daily ritual can help us to stay grounded and connected to ourselves. Taking time to slow down and connect with myself ahead of the day's agenda has brought more harmony to my day. When we make space to sit in ritual and to be fully present and truly honour ourselves, we become more productive and grounded.

HOW I HAVE MY SACRED CACAO

This morning, as I write this, I sit in my Witchy shed at the bottom of the garden cradling my cup of sacred cacao, watching the birds going about their business. I take my first sip and can immediately taste the magical medicine of cacao. As I feel it vibrating through me, I connect and am grounded. I reflect on my intentions for the day, all the while enjoying my time with my lovely hug in a mug. I complete this ritual by journaling and afterwards I feel more in tune with myself. This ritual helps me to achieve my goal of creating some stillness in my life. Life can be so busy, so this is about pausing instead of doing, which gives me the space to feel into what I want to create next. It is my main tool that I use to bring a pause to my day, where I can sit in ritual each morning being fully present with myself. The sacred cacao helps me feel and to listen as I reflect and open my heart to my calling.

The more we practice staying in the present moment and living intentionally, the more this will become second nature and assist you in navigating through the fast-paced lives we lead, staying on track with what we want to create in our life.

To Make Cacao

You can buy cacao as a powder or as a block to grate yourself. I recommend using 20g to 50g of chopped or grated cacao, 100ml to 200ml of your choice of water or plant-based milk, and a natural sweetener, such as raw honey or coconut sugar, if desired.

★ Gently warm your water or milk in a pan.

★ Carefully chop or grate your ceremonial cacao, weigh the amount you want and add it to the pan.

★ Mix the cacao in with a whisk so it melts.

★ Serve in your favourite cup or mug.

Being Present

So what does being present actually mean? It means to step out of your programmed thoughts, to just observe your surroundings and to be fully aware. Let go of thinking, and doing, and simply be in the present moment. Time to be connected to our heart and to our soul.

When we increase our awareness of being present in the moment, we are then able to understand with more clarity the important messages our body is telling us. When we better understand the important messages from our body, we know what we need to do (or not do) in order to create a sense of harmony in mind, body and spirit.

Be more aware, more conscious with your everyday pleasures. Admire the flowers in the vase when you are eating breakfast. Enjoy the sun when you are walking outdoors. Listen to the birdsong and observe the nature that is around you. What experiences give you ease and joy? What gives you a sense of flow? Is it painting, reading a good book, cooking? Take mental note of the activities that give you flow, and consciously aim to do more of them. By feeling joy in little moments we are more rooted to the present rather than dwelling too much in the past or on the future.

We all work from our thinking mind, but we are actually powerful when we listen from the heart space. To connect to this area, we must slow down and be in the present moment. Ask and listen. Feel into the vibrations of the answers we are seeking.

The mind is so busy running around taking care of what's going on outside that it doesn't hear the heart. The heart is the connection to our soul, it is our anchor into meaning and truth, and can serve as our compass and guide in times of confusion or stress. Our heart is where our true desires lie, not what the head thinks we want but what our authentic self actually needs. When we slow down enough to listen to our hearts, it allows greater clarity to come through. Silencing the noise in the head and listening to the wisdom of the heart leads to a clear mind. When we centre ourselves in our heart, we become aligned with what really matters most to us.

A self-care ritual performed each day means I take time to slow down and connect with myself ahead of the day's agenda, bringing more peace to my day. When we make space to be fully present with ourselves and to honour ourselves, we become more productive and grounded, allowing us to then lead with the heart. I have felt more deeply attuned to myself, more energetic and mentally alert.

In times of stress or upset, our hearts may become closed. When we open our hearts, it can help us cope in challenging times. The first step is to notice yourself, to check in and be mindful in each and every moment. Being who you are, being more present, responding to each moment as it comes.

If you stop thinking about the past and only focus on the present and think of your best possible future, then your frequency changes. You start to attract. Don't think of the how, just focus on the present and raising your vibration to attract your best possible future. Being present taught me so many things. I stopped listening to the garbage in my mind and started thinking positively. I also gained self-awareness and self-confidence.

We are receiving information all the time. In order to make real change within our lives, we have to bring the subconscious up to our conscious awareness.

SURRENDER...

You cannot control your thoughts. You cannot control your emotions.

BUT YOU CAN CONTROL HOW YOU RESPOND TO THEM.

Only in stillness can you focus, and receive and use your intuition.

Stepping into Your Present Self

Connect to your breath, get relaxed and grounded, sit comfortably and breathe deeply. Close your eyes and draw your attention to your heart. Breathe deeply. Take a deep breath in and see your heart space as a ball of pure white light. Your soul is always calling and inviting you to return within, to return home. Place your left hand on your heart, close your eyes and focus on your breath and say to yourself:

★ *"How am I feeling?"*

★ *"Where in my body am I holding stress?"*

★ *"I am fully present to my heart space, to my soul"*

★ *"I am enough"*

★ *"I am safe"*

Intuition

I believe that our intuition is our soul speaking to us gently and in my opinion the best form of guidance we have. I simply no longer doubt my intuition because I have learnt that when I follow it, I live my most aligned, authentic version of my life.

Every single one of us has been born with the intuitive gift of 'knowing'. Your intuition is actually trying to feed you information all day, every day. Intuition is a non-stop stream of communication with the subconscious, energetic parts of ourselves. We just need to practice and be still for long enough to hear and feel it.

HOW TO ACCESS YOUR INTUITION

1. Choose a time and space where you can be quiet.

2. Think of a question or an issue you want answers for.

3. Write the question or issue down. Keep it simple and brief.

4. Be in the stillness and feel your feet in contact with the ground. Focus on the area of your heart. Breathe calmly and let your body release any tension.

5. Hold your question lightly in your mind and wait. Don't force anything. Be open to whatever comes. It could be a feeling, words, ideas or thoughts that seem to come out of nowhere. How do I really feel about the whole situation? What do I need to know? What feels like the right thing to do? Don't push, let answers arrive by themselves.

6. Write down anything that will help you remember what came up. Do not think about it, judge or dismiss it.

Like anything, it takes practice. The more time you spend listening to your soul, the easier it is to differentiate between the voice of your head and the voice of your soul. So how does your soul sound? The soul speaks to us subtly – it does not shout; it whispers and is gentle and positive. It speaks to us in feelings, knowings and visions. Every day we are bombarded with messages from the world we live in and the people we surround ourselves with. When we take the time to tune in and receive a message from our soul it feels incredible.

One of the ways I connect to my soul is I light a white candle and sit on the floor connecting to my breath so I slow down my energy. I place my left hand on my heart and ask "what is my soul saying, what does my soul need right now?"

Your heart is your connection to your soul. When your heart gives you a sign or a feeling, this is aligned with your soul and purpose! So don't ignore it. Trusting your intuition is all about trusting yourself. The more you listen to your intuition and follow the signs from the Universe, for example synchronicities, the higher the vibration you create in your life. It is my biggest navigational sign that I use and I rely on them. I never begin anything new unless I have had a sign. Learning to hear your soul is one of the most powerful tools available to us, and will never steer us wrong.

The world is full of amazing opportunities and when you expect the best, that's exactly what you receive. Give yourself permission to have fun every single day and watch how it shifts every area of your life for the better. Life is an adventure that is meant to be enjoyed!

The Work

Through my ongoing quest of looking for ways to grow spiritually, I had to learn and understand more about the world I am living in. The main thing I discovered was that listening to my inner self and being more present day-to-day gave me a truly soul-led life. For me, this means living with intention and bringing awareness to what I'm doing. It's not about living a perfect life or always being balanced, but making a conscious choice about how you want to live.

The starting point for my personal journey of 'doing the work' was to learn to step into my true authentic self and honour my self. I realized it is enough to just be me, and therefore stopped trying to be anything else. This led to a decision that I would no longer be attached to any one outcome, and I learnt to trust my instincts fully and dive into my life. After a very short time, the Universe surprised me with an outcome that was way beyond anything I could have possibly imagined.

Personal development work always circles back to unlearning our beliefs and uncovering the many layers of conditioning we've been taught to believe about ourselves, which is what forms much of our programming. We all have limiting beliefs that are built upon fears and are very much not built on facts.

This section of the book will give you lots of journal prompts to help you with your own self-discovery that you can work through at your own pace. Please be aware that when we look back into our past and examine our beliefs, it can bring up some painful memories. So it's incredibly helpful to ensure you make time for some self-care to accompany this type of work.

I believe that if you really want to change, or really want something, YOU have to set aside the time to make it happen. There has to be commitment as no one is going to do the work for you. Finding spare time can be hard, but like anything, if you want to see the results you have to make changes to your routine. I am still doing the work – and reprogramming is my highest priority.

Create a world you desire to be part of

A large part of my journey so far has involved honouring myself. To honour yourself is to give your inner self love and care, and to allow time to create a personal practice where you can receive inspiration and visualize your dream life. To make this become a reality, you must bridge the gap between where you are and where you want to be. This means taking action, and has led me to:

★ Stepping out of my comfort zone and trying new things without fear.

★ Being truly honest with myself.

★ A much stronger dedication to my path.

★ Development of my gifts.

★ Undertaking shadow work.

You were born into this lifetime for a reason. This lifetime is about figuring out why. Find your gifts, find your purpose and create the life you have always dreamed of.

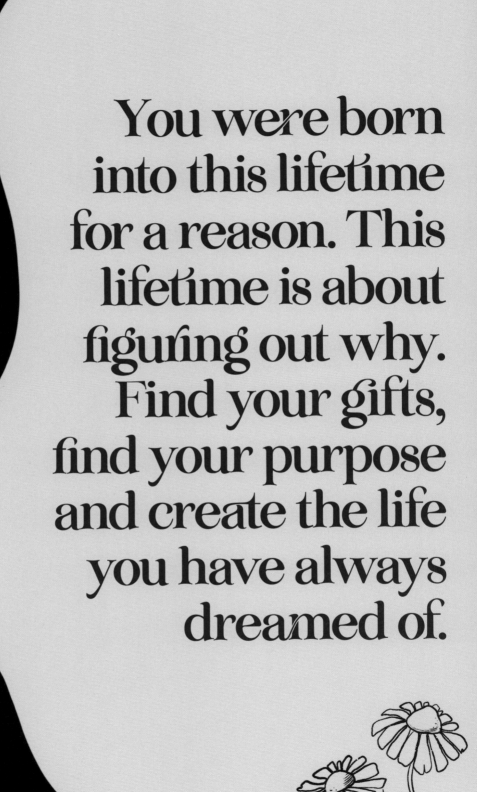

Authentic Self

When your soul came into this world you were completely authentic. Our programming during childhood slowly takes us away from this, so we become mirrors of our upbringing. One of our purposes in life is to return to our authenticity, where we start to really know ourselves again and find our true purpose. It's important to remember that the past was not a waste of time. Every time you find yourself self-criticizing and self-judging, remind yourself that you are exactly who and where your soul chose to be in this lifetime.

How many times do you find yourself saying yes to things that don't light you up, or committing to something you really did not want to do, just to fit in, be liked or loved?

How much of your days, career, choices, thoughts, relationships, interests, items in your home are actually someone else's story that has been mirrored to you.

Now is the time to release all of this and start showing up exactly who you are. Living authentically is prioritizing the things that our soul craves for us to do. THIS is living as our authentic self.

One of the most powerful ways to find your authentic self and step into your true purpose is to mix in a huge virtual 'future' cauldron everything that fires up your heart and soul including all the natural gifts your soul arrived with when you were born. Get out your journal, light some candles, burn some incense and really FEEL the following questions. Do not rush them, ask your heart for the honest answers. We spend most of our time in our head space THINKING about our answers and decisions rather than FEELING them.

Your Values and Passions

★ *What is important to you in a relationship?*

★ *What do you NEED to receive and what do you NEED to give that person?*

★ *Why does your partner light up your heart?*

★ *What do you spend most of your time and energy on?*

★ *What do you do in your life that brings you joy, that fires up your soul?*

★ *What exactly is most important to you?*

★ *What does your soul desire? Do you desire safety? To be loved, respected, protected?*

★ *Think about all the people you spend the most time with. Which of these bring your energy down? Who gives you the most energy when you are with them?*

★ *When you open your wardrobe, does your clothing present a true representation of how you want to show up and to be seen? Or are you following a crowd, blending in or not wanting to be seen?*

★ *Why are you here in this lifetime? This is the biggest question we never ask ourselves.*

★ *What is it that makes you feel the most alive?*

★ *In a day where there is nothing that can distract you, no jobs or chores or anything that has to be done – your ideal day – what do you HAVE to do, like a desire in your heart?*

★ *Make a list of what you visualize the most when you're dreaming about the future. Which subjects? Objects? Things? People? Experiences?*

★ *What are you wishing for or manifesting in order to have the life that makes you happiest?*

Your Gifts

★ *Looking back on your career so far and the jobs you've had, what have you been naturally good at? What came with ease and what did you enjoy?*

★ *Looking back at your life, what compliments have people given you that you found flattering? For example, "you are such a good listener, you give such great advice, you are so kind and nurturing". These are gifts that other people see that you possess, so when they compliment you about these, you should feel flattered not shocked. If someone said to you, "wow, you are so good at maths, you should be an accountant" but you really don't like maths so you feel shocked, that is a talent not a gift.*

★ *What have you always been really good at?*

★ *What comes easy to you but might not come easy to other people?*

★ *If you could do or be anything, anything at all, what would that be?*

★ *How are you being of service?*

★ *Creativity is one of our greatest gifts. Under the title of creativity, what do you think you could do?*

★ *What part of life truly fires up your heart?*

Now, imagine a huge virtual cauldron in front of you, visualize tipping in all of your gifts and giving it a big stir. Then, add in the answers from the values and passions questions and give it another good stir. THAT is your essence, your true self, your authentic self. In order to live this more authentic life, we must fill our days, where possible, using all of our gifts and sticking to our values. Do the things that light up your heart with fire and you will be spending each day as the authentic you, living your true purpose.

Living this way makes day-to-day decisions easier, for example, if you were offered a new job that you would be greatly rewarded financially for, you can use your list and ask yourself:

★ *Does it use my gifts?*

★ *Does it fire up my heart?*

If the answers are no, you can happily decline the offer, knowing that to say yes would not be honouring your authentic self.

Now ask yourself:

★ *What is your soul's purpose?*

★ *How are you serving the world?*

★ *Are you following your dreams and passion?*

I believe we all have a purpose. If we can find out what it is, we can make a difference to the world. You have everything you need to find your passion, make a difference, and live a happy life.

Once you're fully aligned with your purpose, you begin to experience happiness by living each day while fulfilling your true potential and embracing your natural gifts. You will also find aligned relationships in your life.

To simplify:

Your personal gifts (the natural skills and abilities you have), added to your values and passions (things that bring you joy), added to your mission (the way you want to help and serve people the most) equals…

YOUR SOUL'S PURPOSE

Fears

What is the one thing that stops us from living our soul purpose? Fear! Through my daily work being of service to others, I have guided over forty-thousand people into finding their purpose, and each one has experienced the same fears. Fears of being seen, not being worthy, of being judged by others or taking the risk and everything failing. Of being too old or too young, not being qualified or experienced enough.

We need to face these fears head on and allow our hearts to rule instead of our minds, to connect to the present moment and feel!

When we sense these fears come into our minds we have been programmed to think "no, I must not do this" as a way of protecting ourselves. Instead of facing the fear head on and taking action, we stay in the safety and comfort of our limited beliefs and 'what we are used to'.

Fear puts stress on the body, it can bring on anxiety and depression, affects relationships and can even lead to physical illnesses.

We hold fear in our Root Chakra, which deals with survival and becomes blocked by fear. To cleanse this chakra, you have to face what you are most afraid of, and truly let it go.

HOW DOES FEAR APPEAR IN OUR DAILY LIFE?

One of the main ways is through procrastination, always putting your goals off, or spending time thinking about them rather than taking the actions. Another way fear comes up is when you settle for less than you deserve. It's time to stop making excuses and start achieving your dreams. To stop living in fear, you must pinpoint what's causing the fear. Once you have identified the source, you can change your mindset. The first step is recognising that you have a choice.

DEALING WITH FEARS

When feelings of doubt or fear start, I stop what I am doing and thinking, I light a white candle and sit with my journal and a pen and:

1. Identify the fear and then write it down to acknowledge it. Doubts could be that you are not good enough, are going to fail, are not liked or don't deserve it. I spend as much time as necessary working out what is the root of how I am feeling.

2. Then, I change this by asking myself, what's the worst thing that can happen? Where is the evidence that the thing making me feel stressed will actually take place? What would the most empowered version of myself do? Is this choice aligned with my goals and my future self? Am I making this decision based on my own needs, or on what other people expect of me? I ask myself what is the first little step I can do right now to lift me out of this feeling and closer to my dream?

3. When I have slowed myself down and processed the information, I can see that the fear isn't really as big and scary as it felt a few minutes ago. Having acknowledged this, I will read back what I have written, realize it's silly, there is no evidence it will happen like I am fearing, or no one has ever said that to me. I usually then smile, feeling calmer and more in control of the situation.

The next step is to actually face my fear head on and do it anyway!

We have a tendency to use spiritual ideas and practices to sidestep or avoid facing unresolved emotional issues.

I would like to share with you an exercise that I have learnt that helps me when I am in the lack frequency, when my mind is in constant fear, stress and anxiety.

These are my steps:

WHAT:

★ *What does this lack frequency feel like? Foggy, heavy, fearful, stressful…*

WHERE:

★ *Where am I feeling this in my body? Jaw, tummy, chest…*

GRATITUDE:

★ *Think of five things that I am grateful for: family, friends, health…*

Close your eyes, place your hand on your heart and feel the answers.

SEE:

★ *What I appreciate in my life: family, friends, health…*

FEEL:

★ *What does this appreciation feel like? Love, safe, warm…*

Now the frequency has changed, I feel calm, centred and in control.

Anxiety

Anxiety is a daily battle for many. I'm not a medical professional and can only speak from personal experience, but I would like to share a few things that have helped me over the years and that I use daily.

Write it out Empty your mind of the things that are making you feel anxious onto a piece of paper. It's simple but for me it's like therapy. Once I've written it all down, the intensity of my emotions reduces significantly, my head is clearer and I feel in control again. You might find that using a daily journal helps or just write on a scrap of paper when the need arises. There's no right or wrong way to do this but I encourage you to give it a try.

Stay present: Often our minds are filled with worries about the future and concerns about the way we behaved in the past. We waste so much time ruminating over things and wondering how they could have been different. This is one of the reasons why I believe that mindfulness and meditation has had such an impact on my life. When we learn to stay in the present moment our mind becomes calmer.

Breathe: Take a few deep breaths and focus on what you are experiencing in the moment. Mindfulness is a wonderful tool for making your mind feel calmer. It can be particularly useful for introverts when faced with stressful social situations.

Express gratitude: Express love, kindness and deep gratitude at every opportunity.

Many of us are afraid to step out into the world and to reach our desires. Instead, we hold ourselves back, dreaming and waiting for that right time. In order to make our dreams a reality, we need to take action instead of wishing. The best thing we can do for ourselves is to get out there and take action on our dreams.

BREATH WORK EXERCISE

Below is a breathing exercise that will help with anxiety and to ground you back into yourself.

- Begin with a long exhale out of your mouth.

- Place one hand on your belly and one on your heart.

- Breathe in through your nose and out through your mouth.

- Make your inhales and exhales long and smooth.

- Breathe in this fashion for several minutes, until you become very clear and grounded.

- Finish the exercise by placing both hands on your heart and sending gratitude to your body.

Affirmations

You need to change your beliefs to attract what you want. One of the best ways to do that is by listening to affirmations, saying them out loud or reading them. As we focus on these empowering affirmations, speaking, hearing and absorbing them repeatedly, our brains begin to form new beliefs.

I fully recommend reading affirmations to yourself every day. Pick ones that feel good to you. Use your own words to personalize them as well. You need to believe they are coming from you so it's important to use words that feel good and that you'd say. If the word isn't in your terminology, then it won't feel as natural, and it will be harder to impress upon your mind.

Recording affirmations using your own voice and listening to them every day is very powerful. You could listen to other people's recordings, but it's so much more impactful and direct to hear yourself. You don't need any special equipment; I simply use the voice recorder on my phone. I then play them back whenever I get a chance. This method has completely changed how I think.

Affirmations allow us to take control of our thoughts and emotions so that fear does not dictate what we do with our lives. Change how you think about yourself in order to bring more happiness into your life. Here are some affirmations that I use:

- I have the potential to do anything that I want.

- Everything is always working out for me.

- I know that the Universe is abundant.

- I know that I'm coming closer into alignment with what I want.

- I love knowing that I am the creator of my own reality.

- I always have everything I need.

- I am divinely guided and protected at all times.

- I am a powerful creator.

- I invite good feelings into my body now.

- I am a powerful, creative being and I create my life with intention.

- I deserve the best life has to offer.

- I am open to receive what is meant for me.

- I love myself first.

- I create space for those who matter.

- I know my worth.

- I release anything that is not in alignment with my vibrations.

Small Acts of Kindness

While we are doing the work on ourselves, we can also inspire others and help spread kindness through our daily lives. We can make the world a better place by being our true authentic selves.

Despite our fears and limitations and the uncertainty that hold us back, we can still all implement small acts of kindness. Through my own personal healing journey, whenever I stop to help others, I feel a warmth inside that is a tiny part of the affirmative transformations that take place when I make being of service a part of my everyday existence.

As we have already covered, it's really important to make your home space into your self-care container, your own Sacred Space, so you can take what you have learnt into your workplace and share this loving energy. You can be more positive with your thoughts, which will radiate out into the world, give donations of time or money, smile at everyone you meet, and be fully present with those you love and are in need of your assistance.

Simple things like sharing time can be transformative, not just for yourself. Whenever I am with like-minded people and we start sharing ideas together we generate this beautiful positive energy that then serves as the motivation for change.

We are regularly exposed to so much negative energy generated by suffering, personal fears and pain. So selfless, small acts of kindness remind us that we provide some degree of control over a world that can seem chaotic at times. We are capable of changing the world in a positive way.

Shadow Work

In order to live a Sacred Life, you need to heal from the past and unlock the lessons you have learnt throughout your life so far. By doing this, you will discover the ways you've been programmed since birth so that you can let go of what's weighing you down and raise your vibration. This is how you create a life that's in flow and full of joy, which is the Sacred Life!

Shadow work is looking into the shadows of your soul, into the darkness to see what is there, bringing it up to the surface to be released. From the moment we are born, we all receive programming from our parents, the media and from friendships. To unblock this information, you need to trace them back to your childhood and learn the root of where every issue stems from, for example feeling unlovable or unworthy. These are the parts of us that we hide from society, that you'd never want anyone to know about you.

So how does your shadow self appear in your life? Our shadows show up in our lives as negative self-talk and self-sabotage. One of the ways we can see our shadow is through our thoughts and our actions with regards how we talk to ourselves and how we judge other people. When we judge another person it causes a trigger of emotion, we will get judgmental, annoyed and jealous. What we judge in others is a subconscious reaction to what we have denied in ourselves. You see, everything is a reflection in a mirror. Anything you are jealous about in another person is truly a reflection of yourself and it is an invitation for you to step up into your authenticity, and embrace the parts of yourself that feel unworthy.

I came to learn that the things I found triggering about others were, in fact, unresolved aspects in my own life. Noticing that helped set me free!

We all have those feelings of being annoyed at others' success. Stop comparing yourself to others. Take time to appreciate all the good things. When you acknowledge the positives, often more good things will come! Witness others' achievements with excitement, say to yourself, "I am blessed as well and good things are happening to me too."

To spot your shadow, ask yourself:

- Are you judging someone right now?

- Are you feeling envy or jealousy?

- Which things make you judgemental?

Before we change anything, first we have to accept it. Accepting our shadow is an important part of reprogramming. It is a good idea to write these things down to get them out. Write down your fears and what you are afraid to admit to yourself. If you feel overwhelmed then concentrate on just a little shadow work to begin with, spending your time on just one of the following prompts in each journaling session.

- How do you think people see you?

- Where do you feel you are playing small in your life?

- What do you think your shadow is?

- Who in your life made you feel the most shame?

- In what situations are you the most uncomfortable and find it the hardest to be yourself?

- What qualities do you possess that you seem to always have to make excuses for?

- How are these stopping you reach for your dreams?

- How has your upbringing influenced the way you show up for yourself?

- When is the last time you felt let down? Examine how you felt and whether it was truly rational or if you were triggered.

- What makes you feel most valued?

Allow these to come to the surface and feel them. Don't push them away; feel every part of them as that is how they will be released. After you recognize what uncomfortable emotions you've kept hidden from yourself and stuffed down because they are painful, it's time to feel them. When you feel them, you release them.

After you write down your fears, invite these emotions into your body to be felt. This can seem a bit scary at first because you are likely used to pushing them away. After you've recognized and felt your uncomfortable emotions, it's time to love them. Send love to all of your shadow aspects and accept them as part of your experience here on Earth. Thank them for being here because they likely helped you in some way.

There is so much talk about being positive and being happy, which is great, but this work needs to be done as well. If you can't go deep into your soul and look at your shadows, then you will never be able to move forward and be positive and happy. Stuff will keep coming up for you and you won't be able to successfully move forward without looking at these parts of you first.

Sit with them, feel what they are trying to get you to feel and your shadow self will be happy and therefore you will be happier too. You will move forward much more quickly by acknowledging your shadow parts rather than by resisting them.

Your Inner Child

Our childhood wounds and traumas cause blockages. These will affect our lives and also stop us from returning to our authentic self. By working on our beliefs, we can slowly heal our inner child. By reconnecting with who we are authentically, we subconsciously increase our vibration and therefore we become happier.

Your inner child is that deeply sensitive part of you that deserves full attention, protection and unconditional love. It holds emotions, memories and beliefs from the past as well as hopes and dreams for the future. The inner child is always a part of you. If you're feeling frustrated or stuck in some aspect of your life, it's possible that your inner child is needing some attention. These stuck points can look like difficulties at work, in parenting, finding love, deepening relationships or setting boundaries.

This little version of yourself holds some of your most impactful memories, especially the ones that reveal your soul purpose. The Universe is also encouraging you to think back into your childhood and remember those moments that brought you excitement, joy and opened your heart chakra for the first time, to things that inspired you.

Through journaling, ask yourself the suggested questions and the answers will help guide you back to your purpose.

INNER CHILD JOURNAL PROMPTS

★ When you were a child, what did you want to become as adult? Have you fulfilled that? Did your dream change?

★ What did you love to do as a child?

★ What were you naturally very good at as a child?

★ If you were sitting in front of your child-self right now, what would you say to them? How would you treat them? What do they look like? How do you view them? Does this affect how you look at yourself now as an adult?

★ Describe what your childhood was like in one sentence. Was it generally happy?

★ What's one thing you wish you could change about your childhood?

★ How can you nurture your creativity now as an adult?

★ What do you have negative self-talk about?

★ What makes you feel anxious? Where do these feelings stem from?

★ In which areas of life do you hold yourself to an unachievable standard?

★ What grudges are you holding on to? How can you let them go?

★ Do you prioritize yourself?

★ Name a time that you forgave yourself for messing up.

★ What is your first memory of feeling ashamed?

★ How did shame become part of your self-talk?

★ Who around you shames you?

★ When you feel ashamed, how do you react?

★ Who inspired you as a child?

★ Write a letter to someone from your childhood self to thank them for being there for you.

★ What do you wish your childhood self knew that you know now?

Limited Beliefs

In my opinion, limited beliefs are the biggest obstacle to feeling truly happy. You were not born with limited beliefs, they come from your childhood programming. When we are young, we are told and experience certain things. Our parents, siblings and others in our environment tell us what they like, what they believe, and offer their opinions. During this period of our growth, we are trying to figure out how life works, trying to figure out how to be accepted, how to find approval. Our world around us, surrounded by the people we love and look up to, become like mirrors as to how we should be and act, because we crave their love, affection and approval. We grow up never questioning these beliefs, even though it's not necessarily how we feel.

Limited beliefs will stop you from going after the things you are wanting in life, for example:

• That dream job you are wishing for – you could possibly think you are unworthy to get such a position.

• That perfect partner you wish to have in your life – you may think you can only attract a certain type and it always goes wrong, or that you are unlovable, even that there is something wrong with you.

• From launching that business because you just assume you can't do it or will fail.

These limited beliefs lead to limiting decisions. They stop us from doing the things we want to do and stop us from leading the life we want. A good way to know if it is a limited belief is to ask yourself how it feels. If it makes you feel bad, or inadequate and unworthy, it is a limited belief.

Overcoming these limited beliefs can start with a simple inquiry. Ask yourself:

"Is this true?"

"Where is the evidence of this?"

Finding your belief and values allows you to break the limited thinking. They will help you get to know who you are, build confidence within yourself and feel like you're living an authentic life. Knowing what is true for you is the biggest action for taking control and living a happy life.

In my experience, holding onto the pain rooted in the past really doesn't help your present, let alone your future. After unlocking your past, it is good to let go and forgive, as this energy isn't serving you and is very negative. Forgive everything and everyone, let go of your judgments so you can begin to form more positive thoughts and emotions. What I have learnt is we can't control all of the circumstances we find ourselves in, but we can choose how we feel about everything.

To heal from this, you can rewrite your beliefs into positive ones. Over time these new beliefs will become the vibration. On one page in your journal write down all the limited beliefs you feel you hold right now. Rewrite your beliefs into positive ones on the opposite page. For example, if you think "I can't get that opportunity that I want," then opposite this write, "I am more than enough and deserving to get this opportunity that I want."

Each morning for 21 days read the new beliefs you have entered into your journal, so they act as affirmations.

Self

Now we have created our home container that will help facilitate our wellness and committed to having a spiritual practice, we need to continue this soul-led path into our daily life in our homes, careers and lifestyles.

Our daily life can be stressful with everything we interact with and the people who surround us, so we do not want our good work of raising the vibrations to be ruined by these external stresses.

To avoid situations and negative individuals who may bring us down, the best course of action is to reconnect to the present and make decisions from your heart space, never from your mind space. The mind space uses information learnt throughout your life and programming so far, whereas the heart space is our true self, our soul, which is where the decisions that you feel are right for you come from. It only wants the best for us, so we must learn to trust what it tells us and know this is right. This means we can sometimes disappoint others, which can then bring up fears of rejection, but we must not let this sway us; follow your heart, it will guide you in the right direction.

During my busy life as a photographer, I would often get asked questions or to do certain things on a photo shoot that I would not feel a strong answer about. My little trick was to not rush into an answer, pretend that I needed the toilet and go to the bathroom to receive the guidance needed for the situation.

I would then close my eyes, place my left hand on my heart, connect to my breath and centre myself.

I would ask my soul how do I FEEL about the situation. Do I want to say yes or no? Then, after hearing my soul, I would go out and speak my truth from a place of love, knowing that it was the right decision.

As you can see, it all goes back to the spiritual practice of being present, being still, asking and receiving in trust.

Conscious Motherhood

As a psychic medium, I have spoken to hundreds of different spirits throughout my life. So many of the chats have been about the spirit world, what is it like, how it works, and there have been many conversations around reincarnation and souls. A beautiful thing they have explained is how our children chose us, they pick us to be their parents and come to Earth in order that they can live out their soul's contract.

I am a mother of two children, who are now adults who have left the nest. While my kids were growing up I made it my mission to always show them compassion and understanding. I wanted them to have great confidence and embrace their experiences in the spiritual realm. There ARE ghosts. There ARE spirits. As far as I'm concerned, there are even aliens. As parents, it isn't our place to discount anyone else's experiences. Even though we don't have all the answers, it's important to acknowledge what our children are feeling. It's amazing how much of a difference you can make in a child's life if they have even one person believing them!

Most children see and hear spirits, so I have always been open to my children talking to me about this, acknowledging and discussing what they experience is so important. When my daughter first started to walk, she would often be seen playing with spirits, interacting with them and doing things I knew she'd not been taught yet. When she started speaking, she would talk about photographs of my family in the spirit world as though she knew them.

At the age of three, my son told me all about his 'other Mummy and Daddy'. He talked about the war and what happened to him with great detail, the things he told me were way beyond the knowledge of a boy who was too young to even understand what he was saying. During these moments, however 'odd' they might have seemed, I always made sure I never discounted their experiences and views.

When my children were younger, they would have dreams that would wake them up. So I always held a space to listen to them. I have taught them that dreams can teach you things. How dreams are your subconscious trying to bring feelings to the surface, encouraging us to pay attention and release.

I've introduced crystals into their lives and placed a few in their rooms. I have educated them about energies and that we can attract positivity by using crystals. Children always seem to love crystals, so it is a great place to start when teaching them about energy. The most important lesson I've given my children is the importance to sit with yourself and just breathe, teaching them meditation is the best thing and is, in itself, the spiritual practice.

It's possible to change the world around us simply by how we raise our children.

Every single parent is a mirror to them. We mirror how to behave and how to think.

Now, I am not the perfect mother by any means, I don't think anyone can be. We all make mistakes, part of the journey is

learning for ourselves and they, of course, have to make up their own minds and have their own opinions. I remember saying in front of my daughter "I can't wear that as I will look fat." Seeing her reaction to that remark made me feel awful! I knew then in that moment that if I could not empower myself, there was no way I could empower her and that I needed to mirror positive body image.

As another example, the world mirrors to men to be strong, to be manly and to not cry as that is a sign of weakness. I did not want this for my son, so instead I've mirrored to be confident in himself, to be able to show his emotions and that it's okay to cry.

Awareness is the key. When we use negative words to describe ourselves, we start to act in ways that prove that we are right because our subconscious can't differentiate between truth and lies. The next time you hear yourself think badly or you speak badly about yourself, STOP, take a moment to pause and choose a new thought to replace it. The more you do this, the easier it becomes and you will mirror the truth.

I believe that children are divine beings of light who have chosen you to love them and help guide them on this earth path. You can really help them by aligning their souls' highest calling and deepest hearts' desires. Include your children in regular spiritual practices such as meditation, simple rituals, teaching the universal principles and sharing your knowledge. As parents we have a job to do – we are here to guide our children onto their path. We are here to help awaken the wisdom that is already within them.

Our daughters deserve to be taught that it is absolutely necessary to prioritize their needs, to put themselves first, to set boundaries, not to feel ashamed or guilty to ask for and receive support. It is important to teach our children about the importance of self-care.

Self-care isn't about face masks and massages! There is a belief that self-care activities cost a lot of money, and require you to leave your house, which may seem unrealistic and unattainable for many women in current times.

- It is about stopping throughout the day to breathe and be fully present so you can connect to your higher self.

- Waking up half an hour before the rest of the household and making a cup of tea to drink alone in silence.

- Meditate for 10 minutes in the morning and write out a gratitude list.

- To put away your phone and unplug from the heavy energy of social media and the news.

- To go for a walk or a run, wind down with a night-time yoga session or sweat it out to some cardio and strength training.

- To nurture your body with your favourite food.

- To clean and get rid of things from your house that have no use to you anymore and no longer bring you joy.

- To journal about your feelings, to give yourself permission to feel it all!

Self-Love

How we talk and feel about ourselves really impacts on our beliefs and personal vibrations. We are often very harsh and beat ourselves up with negative feelings, for example about how we look.

This bad energy affects everything in our lives: it makes us more stressed, less happy, anxious, depressed, stuck and more likely to reach for a distraction that will comfort us from the stress of being who we are.

Self-love is:

• Talking to yourself with love.

• Prioritizing yourself.

• Giving yourself a break from self-judgement.

• Trusting yourself.

• Being true to yourself.

• Being nice to yourself.

• Setting healthy boundaries.

To practice self-care, we need to go back to the basics and listen to our bodies, eating healthily, but sometimes indulging in your favourite food, taking risks, setting boundaries or doing something creative. This goes back to our authentic self and your authentic self work.

Ways to practice self-love are:

• Becoming mindful – feeling instead of thinking.

• Taking actions based on desires.

• Making room for healthy habits.

• Being true to yourself, which goes back to the question, does it fire me up?

Choosing to fall in love with who you are is a powerful act of self-love. When you fall in love with yourself you begin to see yourself more positively, to appreciate your unique outlook on life and treat yourself in a more nurturing way. If you feel really good about yourself it is impossible to have bad thoughts. You will eventually block out all bad thoughts and negative emotions so that every day will be an uplifting and happy experience. You are giving yourself one of the greatest gifts you have to give. You are giving yourself the gift of your love. You are honouring yourself.

When you start to honour yourself and start to do the work, you will grow spiritually.

You will no longer look back at the past full of regret because you understand that it is all part of the journey of getting to where you are now. You may notice that your friendship circle will change because you are wanting like-minded people around you who support you and lift you up, rather than the draining or negative energy of those you may have surrounded yourself with before. The most beautiful part of growth like this is that you stop wasting time on the things that no longer serve you and instead you step into what lights you up and fires up your heart. It is all part of the journey of returning you back home to yourself, to crave deeper connection and meaning into your life.

Part of honouring yourself is holding space for your own self-care. Healing can be very heavy and exhausting, so I recommend a bath ritual to relax the body and nurturing the heart space.

Bath Ritual

YOU WILL NEED

- Candles – to dim the lights and make a calm Sacred Space.

- Sea salt – to eliminate toxins, neutralize negative energies and receive minerals.

- Lavender essential oil – to strengthen and calm your mind.

- Flower petals – to boost inner beauty and reconnect to your inner goddess.

- Amethyst crystals – to boost your intuition and balance your mind.

- A drink – to hydrate during your bath.

METHOD

1. Run your bath with self intentions of healing, adding your ingredients.

2. NO PHONES!

3. Give yourself enough time to fully relax and meditate in your ritual bath water.

4. Wash away any negativity and allow new healing energy to wash over your body.

5. Visualize yourself being cleansed from head to toe.

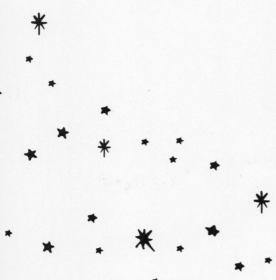

YOU are the most important person in your life – so honour yourself! When you look in the mirror, say I love you. Be kind to her. Say gentle words and honour her. It's not selfish, because when you honour yourself you become a better girlfriend, wife, mother, sister.

My vibration is high because of how I live my life, how I do my self-care, how I take care of my mind, body and spirit.

Bringing peace to yourself is part of self-love. Peace means to me:

- Staying home.

- Being with my husband, kids and doggies.

- Drinking my Sacred Cacao.

- Meditating.

- Deep conversations.

- Listening to my dogs snore.

- Holding crystals.

- Connecting to my guides.

- Silence.

- An organized home and rearranging my furniture.

- Lighting incense/smudging.

- Shopping for plants.

- Laughing with my husband.

- Being grateful.

Style

We have started to talk about the spiritual self but did you know that our clothing can also help our energy? I have always loved fashion; I actually started my career at 19 as a fashion designer. During this time, I had a love/hate relationship with the industry. I saw how much waste fast fashion created in the world, the costs involved and profit!

It made me more aware of how much of an impact this can have on our planet. We all need to bring a deeper awareness into our consumer habits, to really understand why we believe we need so much stuff to be happy.

Over the years, I went through many different styles, from wearing clothes I thought would make me look more professional, to fitting in with everyone else and basically blending in. I realized that this is not authentic to my soul, so I had to look within and really see who the real me was. This transformation has changed my life, and my relationship with clothes has shifted from a mass consumer to a deeply spiritual practice.

Clothes hold an energy, and when we dress with intention, we set the energy into what we are seeking to embody. The colours you choose to wear, the style you go for, all have some kind of effect on the way you carry yourself throughout the day. Chakras are important here too. Say, for example, you're about to give a public speech, opting for shades of blue, which is the colour of your throat chakra, might help you take the stage with confidence.

It's taken me a good five years to adjust my wardrobe to reflect my true self, but I have never felt more in alignment with my true authentic style. I'm no longer led by fashion trends, instead I tune into what I want to wear and what makes me feel good. Rather than buying because I think I should have it, I make my purchases with intention.

Here are some tips on how to shop more consciously:

- Buy vintage or second hand.
- Buy from ethical and sustainable brands.
- Swap clothes with your friends.
- Let go of an item from your wardrobe every time you buy something new.
- Buy from local businesses who are also trying to make a difference.

When I open my wardrobe now, the best way I can describe what I see is a row of yumminess! Every item empowers me, I feel amazing in each item of clothing, therefore I radiate that energy out to the world. I have been very conscious when buying the items so that they are made from beautiful fabrics that will last a lifetime.

It is all about raising your own vibration. After your morning practice, think about how you want to feel during the day. Then pick an outfit to embrace that energy.

So many of us walk around going about our daily life looking down and not engaging with others. I feel it is important to radiate energy out, for us to look at people in the eye and smile! You could be the only person that smiles at them all day. So make a difference, radiate positive energy wherever you go. Ask yourself as you get ready to leave the house, what kind of energy do I want to radiate out today?

Positive Thinking

There are many self-help books mentioning the importance of being positive. I believe that it is hard to be positive all day every day, but we can commit ourselves to living more positively. We can be more aware of our thoughts and we can reprogram ourselves to become more happy and at peace. So spiritual practice is the best starting point for this process and there are more ways to bring positive thinking into our daily lives that will help us raise our own energy and have more clarity and peace.

The one thing you have to realize is that there will always be both negative and positive elements in your life, but you have the power to control which ones affect you. Taking control of your mindset can change your outlook on situations to something more positive.

Everything in the Universe is made up of energy that all vibrate at different frequencies. We are all energy and we are all connected to each other. The higher your vibration, the happier you feel, in turn your happiness can radiate out to others.

There are many ways you can raise your vibration when you are feeling low.

Breathe. As a society we are constantly rushing from one thing to the next. Daily breath work will help you be in the present and calm your nerves. Slow down and really focus on your breathing. Breathe in through your nose and feel your breath go all the way down your body, breathing out through your mouth and letting out a sigh – releasing all the energy that no longer serves you.

High vibration foods will help keep your vibes high! When you make food at home and you use clean ingredients, you know exactly what goes into your body. Everything you eat has an energy of its own. Set intentions while you cook. Your energy when preparing your meals also matters;- it's adding an ingredient of love to your cooking.

Pay attention to what you consume. The things we watch on TV, read about and see on social media all carry a vibration. Be aware of the things that trigger a negative reaction in you. If the news is stressful, step away from it. If your social media is full of negativity, unfollow the accounts that do not inspire you. You have the control.

Starting the day with gratitude can literally raise your vibration. There is always something to be grateful for. Take pauses throughout your day to raise your awareness around new things that you notice. Keep a gratitude journal and add new things to it daily.

Connecting with nature is one of my favourite ways to raise my vibration. Going outside for a walk, sitting and reading under a tree, laying down and mediating at a park, taking off your shoes and walking around barefoot, simply sitting by a creek and listening to the sounds around you. Find a spot that you are drawn to, then be still in that location and listen to the sounds. Tune into the life that surrounds you and notice the smell of the plants, the temperature, the variety of colours and textures. Close your eyes and breathe with the trees.

It is so important to surround yourself with those who lift you up, celebrate your success and bring you joy. You have committed to your spiritual practice, which means you have begun to honour yourself, but in order to keep your high vibe you must protect your energy. Some people can drain you and take this energy away. These are not your people. Choose those who come into your life that recognize your light, allow you to shine and be your true self.

Find magic in the mundane, turn everyday actions into meaningful rituals by upping the magic factor a notch or two. Stir intentions for the day into your morning coffee or let go of what no longer serves you by moonlight.

Seek out activities that bring you joy. Do one thing that brings you joy each day. This could be a lovely meal out, a cup of coffee with a friend or taking a long bath and meditating. You could have a day of self-care by treating yourself to having your hair done or a massage. Find what brings joy for YOU. Pay attention to the joy that comes up when you participate in an activity that aligns with your authentic values. Compare that to other activities you fill your day with.

Be aware of how you are spending money. Are you buying things that will light up your heart or maybe improve your own Sacred Space? If you buy clothing will it last or is it throw-away fashion? Are you buying something to try to fix a negative feeling?

Save up and treat yourself to something that lights a fire inside and brings you joy when you see it, and celebrate you!

Learn the power of NO! Create boundaries, say no to the things you know do not align with what you value.

Boundaries

Through my own personal development, I have learnt how to set healthy boundaries and come to understand that doing this is an act of self-love. Loving yourself means that you stand up for yourself even if other people don't like it. I believe that setting healthy boundaries is very important for protecting your own energy.

If you constantly give without receiving, then your energy will be off. This will affect you and have a knock-on effect with other people, which can then in turn impact on humanity as a whole, then spreading out into the Universe.

Setting healthy boundaries in both your work and personal life is an act of love and it isn't selfish to do so. It's basically another of the main ways of giving yourself self-care as you are honouring and putting yourself first. Boundaries are really important to give us a sense of safety and how we function in our lives. They are parameters we put in place in order to know that we have guidelines on how to operate, for asking for what we want, and for trying to satisfy our needs.

When we put a boundary in place, we are saying to ourselves that we respect what we need and want, and that we are asking others to respect the same. This can help develop more clear communication and relationships with anyone in our lives.

It's not about pushing people out of our lives or keeping them at arm's length. It's informing yourself and others around you about what you need to have healthy relationships. Boundaries give us the space to operate our lives in a way that feels safe.

In fact, healthy boundaries actually help us achieve more intimacy. When you feel safe in your relationships and within yourself, you enhance your ability to be clear, to share with your partner or those important to you and to build a deeper bond. Don't think of boundaries as keeping people out. Think of them as defining spaces that allow you the freedom to play, think, create, grow, learn, and enjoy life on your terms.

We want to make sure we don't create boundaries out of anger, defensiveness or negative emotions. Healthy boundaries aren't about getting revenge or proving anything to anyone.

Emotions can be difficult to sort through when personal boundaries are not in place.

Make sure that when you create boundaries, your energy feels clear and you are as confident as possible. This will allow you to make a positive plan to engage with the world.

From this place, you can give conscious thought to what your healthy boundaries will be and ensure that they are manageable for you.

Journal a list of your healthy boundaries. Make a list for your relationships, a separate one for your workplace and another for your family and friends.

For me personally, I set boundaries and commit to this lifestyle because it is important for me to stay in as high a vibration as possible.

The Universe responds to our vibrations. It doesn't recognize your desires, it only understands the vibrations, the frequency that you radiate out. When we radiate in fear, stress or guilt we attract more of this vibration. If you are vibrating on a higher frequency of happiness, peace and abundance, you will attract more of that frequency.

Try to be a little more conscious about your thoughts. What thoughts do you give your attention to throughout the day? Do you get stuck in the negativity? Every time you have a thought that brings you down, try to turn it around by thinking about something positive. You will feel your energy change.

I want to inspire you to be fully present as much as possible. Even when you are at work, find those small moments of stillness, or when you are on a trip out, stop and be fully present in your surroundings. Life is an adventure that is meant to be enjoyed! Give yourself permission to have fun every single day and watch how it shifts every area of your life for the better. The world is full of amazing opportunities and when you expect the best, that's exactly what you receive.

The biggest change I have experienced since keeping my vibration high is that I now experience hardly any stress, which in turn makes me happier.

When I raise my own vibration, all my stress, worries, frustrations and problems genuinely just fade away, which leaves me with all the juicy experiences my HEART craves, such as abundance, freedom, happiness, clarity, LOVE and peace of mind, which all then show up in my reality. When I'm aligned with my soul, I breathe easily, words come to me without over-thinking and people resonate with my energy. I feel safe, calm and in the flow with whatever is happening around me. When I'm out of alignment I feel stuck, weak, tired, anxious and annoyed.

Empowerment Exercise

Here is a visualization technique you can try when your life leaves you feeling overwhelmed. You can start in the morning and repeat any time as needed.

- Begin by taking a few moments to breathe deeply and relax.

- When you are calm and present, envision a ball of light in your solar plexus area just above your belly button.

- Allow it to build there, growing stronger and stronger.

- Eventually, allow the light to expand throughout the rest of your body until it fills your entire body and energetic field.

- Place your left hand on your heart and say, "I call back my power, this is not my energy to hold." Repeat this saying three times.

- By filling yourself with your own energy in this way, you become one with your own power.

I call back my
power, this is not
my energy to hold!

I call back my
power, this is not
my energy to hold!

I call back my
power, this is not
my energy to hold!

Grief

Nothing is constant, change is something that happens each and every moment in our lives. The act of grieving is a natural process. It allows us to sort through the range of emotions that are present. In grief, you may feel it's easier to involve yourself in activities that take your mind off your sadness, but this will only make the route to healing more difficult.

Whenever we lose somebody we love, it is important for us to take time out for ourselves and truly feel the weight of what we are experiencing. It is okay to FEEL. Unless we listen to where we are in the moment, feel all those emotions we experience, they will grow in intensity and they will manifest themselves in less comfortable ways. Once we consciously acknowledge that these emotions are present, we are more able to heal the pain.

In grief, we must allow ourselves to accept and deal with our loss fully. Then we will be able to continue our life's journey with a much more positive outlook. The grief journey doesn't have to be rooted in pain, sadness and fear. By understanding that this is part of our daily existence, that there will not only be gains but also losses in our lives, it can help us accept whatever happens.

Here is my personal advice for dealing with grief, which you may find useful in difficult times.

Don't try to run and hide from your grief. You need to experience the pain and sorrow to be able to move past it. Grief cannot stay hidden deep within you. The best way to work through grief is to let it out. Cry, scream and yell if you need to. Express your feelings through music, art or writing. Or express grief with a safe person you love as expressing your feelings is the only true way to honour your grief. Allow yourself plenty of time to do everyday activities and don't over-schedule yourself. Rest when you need to, be gentle on yourself.

AND

It's okay to find joy and fun. Laughter is an excellent medicine. A great way to have some genuine fun is to surround yourself with children or animals.

To help you deal with potentially overwhelming feelings of grief, you can use this following breath work exercise, which I actually use almost every day.

I energetically centre myself by sitting and connecting to my breath, inhale deeply and exhale deeply three times. I consciously call in the highest good of light and guidance. I take a relaxing breath and allow my awareness to flow to my heart space. I breathe and relax my mind and my body.

When I feel stressed, I stand barefoot outside to connect to my breath. Inhale deeply and exhale deeply three times.

8 Small Rituals for Grief

★ Lighting a candle at certain, special times of the day or week to remind you of your loved one (for example, at dinnertime to represent sharing meals with them).

★ Creating a memory scrapbook and filling it with photographs, letters, postcards and notes.

★ Spending time listening to your loved one's favourite music or creating a special playlist of music that reminds you of that person.

★ Watching his or her favourite movie.

★ Planting a tree or flowers in your loved one's memory.

★ Creating a work of art in your loved one's memory.

★ Preparing and eating a special meal in honour of your loved one.

★ Developing a memorial ritual for your loved one on special days or whenever you wish.

The Soul

One of the most important spiritual lessons I have learnt is that the guidance you seek comes from within – from our soul. Our soul truly knows us the best! As an energetic being you signed a contract to be here right now in this lifetime. So your soul knows where you have been and where you are going. Our soul is always guiding us on the highest potential path. The soul speaks through all of your senses. All you have to do is to become fully present with yourself to listen and become aware of its presence and guidance. When you allow the soul to fully lead, you will feel balanced and guided in every area of life.

Simply continuing to connect and follow the guidance of my soul, and the direction these moments have led me, helps me to know that I am living my soul's purpose.

Practice connecting with your soul each day. Just be with it. Ask questions, and notice how the answers come. Try the exercise opposite as an easy way to connect to your soul.

Take a deep breath, feel your feet connect to the earth.

Feel the earth's energy move up through your body into the heart space.

Expand up through the top of your head to connect with the Universe.

Bring that universal light back down through your head to the centre of you.

Gather this energy from the earth and the Universe into your heart space.

Allow that light to grow and build. The brightest part of this light is the seat of your soul.

Visualize it, feel it.

Empowerment Spell

This spell is to banish negative feelings and those limited beliefs within yourself.

You will need:

- 2 pinches of dried rose petals

- 5 whole cloves

- A pinch of dried thyme and rosemary

- A pinch of frankincense resin

- A mortar and pestle

- Charcoal disc

- Heatproof dish or cauldron

1. Feel your guides around you and close your eyes to visualize self-love within.

2. Blend the herbs and resin using your mortar and pestle in a clockwise direction.

3. Connect to your guides and allow them to tell you how incredible you are, how powerful you are and how loved you are.

4. Light the charcoal disc in your heatproof dish and add all the herbs.

5. Say the following:

I am enough,

I am powerful,

I am incredible and
the power within
me is strong,

I am ready to step
into my power.

Rituals

Rituals are intentional actions done in a way that symbolize something much more than the acts themselves. It holds a strong purpose. It involves our emotions and our full attention.

Rituals can be made out of the most mundane acts in your daily life, such as having your first coffee of the day sitting in your garden, getting ready for work in the morning, preparing the evening meal, lighting a candle at the start of the meal or winding down for the evening, having a bath and getting ready for bed. It could be a more specific routine like how we make our beds each morning. We may have a Christmas ritual that we picked up from our parents that we have carried on into our own family unit.

In our fast-moving world, we often miss the good things in our lives. Rituals help ground us and keep us focused with purpose. They can provide an emotional way to celebrate good news. When did you last congratulate yourself? Create a ritual to remind yourself to celebrate small victories.

When I perform rituals, it brings me a sense of deep meaning and purpose. Rituals help me become more in tune with what is truly meaningful.

Rituals can help us cope with some of the most challenging periods of our lives. They are particularly wonderful for families, as we bring together the members of the family into a Sacred Space. When we come together like this and create a family ritual, we can bless what we have in our lives, we can learn to appreciate each moment and gain happiness from living in the fullness of the present. This also, in my view, helps our children make better sense of the world. It is all about those sacred moments of connection, which remind us of the sacred nature of this life.

The Wheel of the Year

The Wheel of the Year provides us with a calendar and rituals that align with nature, helping guide us to connect with the earth by working with eight important days known as sabbats. By noticing the sabbats in the Wheel of the Year we can slow down, reflect, give gratitude and set intentions for what we are working towards. For me, it's a calendar that helps keep me on track with my general lifestyle, but also a great reminder to take things more steadily and be more present in my life.

The sabbats are: Yule (Winter Solstice), Imbolc, Ostara (Spring Equinox), Beltane, Litha (Summer Solstice), Lughnasadh (Lammas), Mabon (Autumn Equinox) and Samhain.

There is a range of possible dates for each sabbat – this is because the equinoxes and solstices happen at precise moments in time, meaning they can fall on different dates in different parts of the world, and the date can vary from one year to the next.

There are two equinoxes in every year, when the sun crosses the equator, and we have equal length of day and night. Working with the Wheel of the Year provides a container for releasing, re-balancing and setting intentions ready for the next new cycle of change.

As a witch, I use the Wheel of the Year in a different way. The start of the year for me is Yule in December, reflecting on what has passed and focussing on what is coming. I work with the winter's energy, letting go of what no longer serves me, getting ready for the year ahead, slowing down and taking time to focus on self-love, so I start the New Year refreshed. As spring arrives, it brings a new energy of excitement and this is an ideal time for setting intentions and manifesting. As summer comes in, this marks for me the mid-way point of the year, the perfect time to check in with myself, give gratitude and celebrate everything I have achieved. As we move into autumn, that's when I start the process of reflecting and honouring.

The following rituals have been created to be easy for you to do, and will hopefully inspire you to adapt them or come up with your own. There is some information about each sabbat and traditionally what you can use on your altar.

When you do a ritual to mark each sabbat, you will feel connected more deeply with the world around you throughout the seasons. You naturally fall into the present moment by actually noticing the seasons changing, notice the world around you and focus on your intentions by looking inwards. I find when we celebrate the cycles of the seasons it gives me a new opportunity for a fresh start, a chance to start over and have a feeling of rebirth.

Yule

Yule, or the Winter Solstice, is when we reach the darkness of the longest night of the year. It is a time of healing and regaining our own personal energy. As we celebrate the longest night and the return of the light, the new energy brings us hope and promise. These dark, cold winter days and nights are inviting us to rest, to stay at home to collect new energy and prepare for spring to come.

Yule for me is all about reflection, family time and stillness before the madness of Christmas Day. I work with Yule by gathering as a family and sharing our intentions as we go inward to reflect on the year and look to what we want to bring into the new year ahead. For me, it is a time to let go. It is a great time to build a Yule altar with collections of natural treasures such as pine cones, evergreens, wreathes, a yule log and a candle to symbolize the return of the light. Spend time embracing the quiet darkness of the season.

Yule

20th to 23rd December

Altar decoration: Bells, candles, evergreens, lights, holly, mistletoe, pine cones, snowflakes, wreaths, yule log, mistletoe, oranges.

Crystals: Clear quartz.

Colours: Red, white, green, gold.

Herbs and flowers: Evergreens, ivy, rosemary, sage, nutmeg, mistletoe, cinnamon.

Oils: Cinnamon, peppermint, frankincense.

Rituals: Honouring family and friends.

Customs: Wreath making, Yule logs, candles and lights, gift-giving, singing, feasting, resolutions and bonfires.

Ritual: Letting Go

A great ritual to do with family and friends. Create a feast and decorate your table so that it holds space for reflection. Each member at the table has a white candle. Make sure the room is dimly lit. Before you start your feast, get everyone to light the candle in front of them. Close your eyes and feel into the year that is about to pass. What are you wanting to let go of, to leave behind as you enter into the new year and a fresh start? Each person around the table states what they wish to let go of and blows out the flame.

Then enjoy your feast but talk as a group about the year that is passing and your achievements, what you are grateful for and what your desires are for the New Year.

Imbolc

Imbolc is a celebration of spring coming and the preparation for the upcoming season of growth. It is typically celebrated with milk and cheeses, lots of candles, and is often associated with the Celtic goddess Brigid. It is a wonderful time to get in tune with the natural rhythm of the seasons and start nourishing yourself with intention and compassion as we step into the season of new beginnings.

Throughout autumn and winter, we naturally and energetically turn within to reflect, heal and rest. Imbolc gives us the opportunity to reflect on that time and integrate the lessons that have come through. A time to look at our inner wisdom and inspiration to plant the seeds of our future growth.

I use this time to go inwards, reflect and focus on self-care. It's a great time to make plans for new ideas, projects and goals that will grow in the spring. We deep clean our home, weed our garden and plan all the things we would like to grow. I like to create an Imbolc altar featuring treasures gathered from nature. Typically these are from the first signs of spring such as flowers that have started to bud, and any new green leaves that have sprouted. Imbolc marks the start of new energy coming back into my body and spirit.

Everything in and around us awakens and is reborn as life begins to stir again. It's an ideal time to put into place some self-care practices that will help you carry out the inspirations and visions you've had through the hibernation of winter and your spiritual growth. Put time in place for self-care as a container of love to guide you through this time.

Imbolc

1st to 2nd February

Altar decoration: Evergreens, white flowers, Brigid's cross, sun wheel.

Crystals: Amethyst, bloodstone, garnet, ruby, turquoise.

Colours: Brown, green, pink, red, white, yellow.

Herbs and flowers: Lavender, rosemary, jasmine, basil.

Oils: Frankincense, rosemary, lavender, chamomile, myrrh.

Rituals: Creative inspiration, purification, initiation, candle work, house and temple blessings.

Customs: Lighting candles, seeking treasures of spring, cleaning house.

Ritual: Self-Love

Place a hand on your heart and focus on a wish for the start of spring. Then, light a white candle while you think about your wish, visualize the light as a warm energy that wraps itself around you, healing your soul, igniting the spark of creativity and cleansing your aura.

Close your eyes for a moment and take three long and deep breaths in and out. Now open your eyes and look at your reflection in a mirror. Allow your gaze to soften and become more loving. See yourself with the eyes of love.

Write in your journal what you are grateful for that your body brings you, what your soul does for you. Find things about yourself that you are grateful for. Love yourself as a divine feminine woman with both shadow and light. Love yourself as the woman who you've always wanted to be.

Ostara

Ostara, the spring equinox, is the first day of spring and represents a time of renewal, balance and rebirth. A time to celebrate the return of the sun, of warmth and of light.

Ostara is the festival of the sun, when day and night are of equal length. After the darker months we are invited to slowly bring about new beginnings, set new intentions, plant the seeds of our desires and welcome in the change of energy. A time to bring passion to our dreams, and spend more time outside. Ostara gives us an opportunity to reflect on our priorities so we can be happier and more productive moving into the lighter months of the year.

Spring is a time of fertility and abundance, the time of the year when the cycle of life, death and rebirth is complete, and we celebrate the rebirth of the soil and the land. Ostara arrives, bringing a warming renewal of all energies. This new energy is an incredible opportunity to set manifestations.

Ostara

19th to 21st March

Altar decoration: Ribbons, eggs, spring flowers, daffodils, tulips, bunny-shaped decorations, baskets.

Crystals: Amethyst, clear quartz, agate, jasper, moonstone, rose quartz.

Colours: Bright green, pink, light blue, yellow.

Herbs and flowers: Daffodils, tulips, narcissus, honeysuckle, peonies, mint, cloves, lemon balm.

Oils: Patchouli, orange, cedar wood, lime, ylang-ylang.

Rituals: Breakthrough, new growth, new projects, seed blessings.

Customs: Wearing green, egg games, new clothes, egg baskets.

Ritual: Set Intentions

I love to create my spring altar, it's definitely one of my favourites. I like to place flowers that I harvested late in the summer and dried. Before the full moon I gather the spring flowers and make blessing bundles to hang up around our home to celebrate the start of spring.

Then, on the full moon after Ostara, I place intentions of the new spring energy into the blessing bundles. You can do this by placing the bundles gently between the palms of both hands and holding them to your heart space. Focus positive energy into them while concentrating your thoughts on all the things you want to achieve in the next couple of months.

OCTOBER

NOVEMBER

I am in alignment
with my desires
and my goals
x

Beltane

Beltane celebrates the height of spring. It's a marker to show the peak of springtime and the beginning of summer. It's during this part of the year when the god and goddess join together in sacred union to fertilize the earth. It's often considered a celebratory period of abundance as nature starts to reawaken with greenery, a time of magic and wonder, when miraculous things seem to happen.

Beltane is traditionally celebrated with bonfires, but the most common image of this sabbat is probably that of the maypole seen on May Day. This celebration of the spectrum of energies within us is when I really anchor into focussing on what I want to birth into this year. What do I want to create, to manifest and how I want to grow spiritually. You can work with this wonderful energy by creating something, for example, starting a new creative project, planting a garden, writing a story, calling in a new relationship or something you wish to manifest into your life.

Beltane

30th April to 1st May

Altar decoration: Spring flowers, green, yellow and blue candles, acorns, cauldron, flower crowns, seeds, wreaths.

Crystals: Rose quartz, jade, opal, tourmaline.

Colours: Pink, green, white, purple.

Herbs and flowers: Daffodils, wild spring flowers, lavender, rosemary.

Oils: Rose, frankincense, jasmine, vanilla.

Rituals: Love, romance, fertility, creativity .

Customs: Maypole dancing, fire jumping, flower baskets.

Ritual: Manifest

Using a candle is a great way to connect to the fire element. This is a wonderful way to bring your desires forward as you work towards your goals. Write your intentions, desires and manifestations on a piece of paper, and be very specific! You can also write an affirmation on there as well such as, "I am in alignment with my desires and goals". Also write HOW they makes you feel. Read this paper out loud as you light the candle. When you are finished with the ritual and have to leave your candle, don't blow it out, instead, snuff the candle so you are not blowing away your wishes.

Colours of candles that you may wish to use:

- Green represents growth, abundance and fertility.

- Red represents strength, vitality, passion and vibrancy.

- White represents cleansing and clearing, and the power to disperse negativity.

- Pink represents love and friendship.

- Yellow represents confidence, communication, joy and business success.

- Black represents protection and absorbs negative energy.

- Blue represents health, protection and calmness.

- Lilac/purple represents psychic abilities.

Litha

Summer's energy is so powerful and uplifting. For many mothers, this is a busy time of the year preparing our children for fun at home and no school. It's also a time for seeing friends, going on holiday and enjoying the outdoors. Summer to me signifies the time when the Earth is at the fullness of fertility and abundance. I like to reflect and focus my attention onto offering gratitude for the abundance that we experience daily.

Litha, the Summer Solstice, falls at the mid-point of the year and is a celebration of light, a time when there is the most light available to us.

This moment in time beckons us to celebrate the beauty and creativity that's arrived into our lives and a time to reflect on personal growth.

During this time, I reflect on my hopes and dreams that were but little seeds and ideas during the dark winter months. During this portal of sunshine, I turn my attention to nature. I kindly connect with the plant spirit and ask for permission before picking them. I then only take as much as I need.

Litha

20th to 22nd June

Altar decoration: Flowers, biscuits, cakes, fruits, white candles.

Crystals: Citrine.

Colours: Green, yellow.

Herbs and flowers: Daisies, roses, mugwort, yarrow, St John's wort.

Oils: Frankincense, lavender.

Rituals: Career, relationships, Nature Spirit communion, planetary wellness.

Customs: Bonfires, all-night vigils, singing, feasting, celebrating with others, making flower crowns, being outside as much as you can.

Ritual: Gratitude

Make a flower mandala by picking flowers from the garden and pulling the petals off to arrange them in circular patterns. The act of creating a beautiful and intentional arrangement using plants is an opportunity to slow down and connect with nature in a new way. As you create your flower mandala, infuse it with your intentions for the season, contemplate your gratitude for life, and hold a vision of wellness for our planet.

Alternatively, write a long journal entry about gratitude from the six months that have passed.

Lughnasadh

Lughnasadh is a celebration of the first grain harvest at the beginning of August. It is a time for gathering and giving thanks for the abundance all around us, for reaping what we have sown throughout the past few months.

Also known as Lammas, this sabbat marks the halfway point between the summer solstice and the autumn equinox. At this point in the year, the days are still longer than the nights, but not for much longer. It offers us a chance to take time to pause, be thankful and celebrate what we have and what we have achieved.

A beautiful way to honour Lughnasadh is to set up your altar and spend time in meditation, connect with your self, take stock of everything you have and then think about what you would like to invite into your life.

Another activity that complements the traditional grain celebration is to bake bread and share it with others, giving thanks for all your abundance. Personally, I love to get together with friends or family for a Lughnasadh feast, marking the high point of summer with good food and plenty of laughter.

Lughnasadh

1st to 2nd August

Altar decoration: Bread, corn, sunflowers, sun, apples, orange and yellow candles.

Crystals: Citrine, carnelian, pyrite.

Colours: Yellow, gold, orange, brown.

Herbs and flowers: Sunflowers, ivy, rosemary.

Oils: Rosemary, sandalwood, rose.

Rituals: Gather flowers to make a bouquet, bake with berries and honey, make corn dolls, bake bread.

Customs: Spend time in nature, practice gratitude, bake bread and leave as an offering in nature or place on altar.

Ritual: Celebration

On this sabbat, I love to take the opportunity to celebrate myself. Us women hardly ever stop and reflect and see how far we have come, so now is a great time to celebrate and honour your accomplishments. I like to treat myself to a beautiful picnic that I take out into nature with my journal. For me, this is a beautiful way to celebrate.

While I am enjoying my picnic, I usually think about three amazing things I have done this year. It doesn't matter how big or small they are, I just sit in the energy of joy and celebration for myself.

I invite you to do the same. Make a beautiful setup for your picnic, grab your journal and pen. Ask yourself:

★ *What does it feel like to celebrate yourself?*

★ *Does it feel uncomfortable?*

★ *Are you coming up with all the things you wish you'd accomplished but haven't yet or all the things you still 'need' to do?*

★ *When was the last time you celebrated yourself?*

★ *Now write in your journal what has come up for you. Step back for a moment while you feel into what you have accomplished. It's time to harvest your celebrations.*

Mabon

The seasons are slowly shifting into autumn with Mabon which falls towards the end of September. This sabbat marks the point of the diminishing sunlight, the time of the second harvest where we celebrate all that has come to fruition from the summer. We are invited to reflect on when we have experienced this abundance in our lives. It is a time of looking at the highs and lows we have journeyed through, knowing that our difficulties have become beautiful lessons when we hold gratitude in our hearts. It is my favourite time of the year.

It is a great time to restore balance in our home by doing a good clean and cleanse, getting rid of anything that you no longer need to make space for inner abundance. It is also the perfect time to go out into nature and find first signs of autumn to bring into your home and altar as autumn decorations. A bonfire is a great way to celebrate the autumnal equinox. Dance, sing, beat drums, play music and celebrate the autumn.

Mabon

21st to 24th September

Altar decoration: Apples, dried corn, pumpkins, herbs, leaves, oak tree sticks, pomegranates, brown and orange candles.

Crystals: Citrine.

Colours: Red, brown, yellow, orange.

Herbs and flowers: Sage, chamomile.

Oils: Frankincense, cinnamon.

Ritual: Prosperity, generosity, continued success.

Customs: Offering of first fruits or grains, games, country fairs, bonfires.

Ritual: Reflection

It is time to celebrate and give thanks for what you have achieved through the year so far. As nature slows down and begins to draw inwards, she encourages you to do the same, moving into your inner world.

Here are some journal prompts to work with:

★ *What am I grateful for so far for this year?*

★ *What has shifted within me since the start of this year?*

★ *What do I desire?*

★ *What can I carry with me for the rest of this year?*

★ *What has this year taught me so far?*

★ *What is holding me back from my dreams?*

★ *What am I wanting to let go of?*

Samhain

Samhain (pronounced 'sow'inn') is one of the major festivals of the Wheel of the Year, and for many pagan cultures the most important festival of all. We celebrate Samhain at the beginning of sundown on 31st October until sundown on 1st November. It is the sacred festival of death, dying and letting go. A time to enter a phase of slowing down, rest, reflection, and dreaming about new beginnings.

This is the time of the year when we can more easily speak with our ancestors as the portal to the spirit world is particularly thin, so it's an excellent time for any kind of divination work.

Samhain

31st October to
1st November

Altar decoration: Acorns, pumpkins, black candles, brooms, cauldron, photographs of deceased loved ones.

Crystals: Smoky quartz.

Colours: Orange, black, white.

Herbs and flowers: Allspice, mint, sage, mugwort.

Oils: Frankincense resin.

Rituals: Honouring ancestors, releasing fears and limited beliefs, foreseeing the future, understanding death and rebirth.

Customs: Pumpkin carving, spirit board, seance, ancestor altar, divination, costumes.

Ritual: Honouring

This is the time we celebrate Halloween. So, during the day, before you do your usual celebrating, create an ancestor altar space. Ancestor altars are a core part of any Samhain celebration. When my children were little, I found this was a great way to tell them about other family members who are in the spirit world, to go through old photos and share memories.

To create an altar, set aside a small space where you can put items that honour your loved ones in the spirit world and a small dish for offerings. Choose somewhere in the home where everyone will gather during the evening. I like to use the lounge as it is the heart of our home. Gather photographs, jewellery, anything from a loved one that you have. Place offerings such as fruit, flowers or pumpkins on the altar. It's good to add in skulls as decoration as skulls symbolize rebirth! You can also leave a few offerings that you know the spirits will enjoy, like black tea, apple slices or wine.

When it comes to old heirlooms or photos, only place items that feel clear and positive to you on the altar. If you want to put something that feels a bit heavy, make sure to surround it with lighter objects, asking them to create a protective circle of healing for both this heirloom and the person connected to it. After you gather and place the items, light a candle in the centre of your altar and let it burn for the evening.

Then in the evening, when your usual Halloween celebrations are done, gather in this space so you can share stories and memories of your loved ones. Give thanks for all the vibrant ancestors in your line and ask for healing for those who might need it.

Birthdays

How often do we women actually celebrate ourselves? Our birthdays are the ideal time to reflect, honour, celebrate and give gratitude, but also to feel into our desires and manifest. After all, birthdays are a celebration of life!

The day before your birthday is a good time to cleanse and do a general declutter. Is there anything you are holding onto that you no longer need? This is a very effective way to get rid of negative energy and allow you to move forward in the coming year.

Ritual

You will need:

12 dried bay leaves

A candle

Matches

A piece of paper, an envelope and a pen

A saucepan or cauldron to burn into safely.

Gather your 12 bay leaves and focus on what you would like to attract into your life in each of the 12 months of the year. Once you are in that focused state and you have felt into your intentions for the year ahead, write a keyword on each of the leaves. Then burn each leaf with a candle on your birthday.

Now sit down at a table with the candle alight and feel into the year ahead. I want you to write a letter to yourself in the present tense such as:

Dear Emma,

This year has been so amazing. I have achieved…

I have loved…

Think about your career, relationships, abundance, family and anything you wish at this point to call into your life. Then finish your letter by stating what you are grateful for in the year that has passed. Seal it in the envelope and keep it somewhere safe. Then on your next birthday, you can open your letter to yourself and see how your wishes have manifested throughout the year.

Grief

Rituals around grief and death have been practiced for centuries and have been a crucial element in dealing with grief and loss.

When someone you love dies, you experience deep, soul-wrenching pain. I personally feel there is nothing sadder than the death of someone/ something you love. Grief is a part of life, however painful, and it's normal. After the first few months of the loss of a loved one, the symptoms of grief can gradually begin to subside, although this isn't the case for everyone and the jouney takes as long as it needs to.

There are things you can do to help grief on its way; one thing I believe can be the most helpful is to engage in ritual. Creating your own personal rituals to remember your loved ones allows you to access and work through your grief in a safe and constructive way. Also see the Grief section in the Self chapter for more ritual suggestions.

Ritual

Before starting the ritual, take a few deep breaths to centre yourself. Remember that it is okay if you cry. This is your space and time to express your grief in whichever ways you need to do so. Create an altar for the person or animal you have recently lost. Place on the altar items that remind you of them, such as photos, objects, their favourite food or even a glass of wine.

Close your eyes and go inwards. Feel all the feels, feel your pain but also go back to happy moments you shared together. Know that their spirit still lives on and that they are always around you. Write in your journal now (even if you are crying) what you are feeling and remembering. Write to your loved one and share how you are feeling. When you need to release your emotions, don't hold back. Yell, scream, whine and cry as much as you need to. Whatever happens in this ritual is completely up to you. This is a healing journey and it doesn't matter how long it takes – there is no right or wrong process.

Conduct your grief ritual for as long and as often as you need to. As you heal, you may find that your need to engage in ritual for your grief will wane.

Remember – all of what was, all that is and all that will be.

About the Author

Emma Griffin was an editorial photographer before becoming the witchy entrepreneur she is today. Emma has dedicated over two decades to her own spiritual growth and wellbeing by living the teachings she shares.

Emma has created a worldwide community through her work as a witch. She is known for her Guidance Medicine Readings®, her sisterhood circles and her lifestyle. Described as down to earth, warm-hearted, compassionate and the real-life Molly Weasley, Emma brings her practices and wisdom to modern day life in a relatable way.

Emma, a mother of two, lives in Cornwall with her husband, six dogs and a cat. Through Emma's life she has gone through several major transformations that have been a huge catalyst for the person she is today. Through her own growth, there was a realisation that she had the power deep within herself. It had been there all along, she just had to learn to look inside herself. Emma learnt that we ALL have everything we need to be happy no matter what we have gone through, or what we have had to overcome.

This is her first book.

Emma shares regular wisdom on Instagram @emmagriffinwitch

Acknowledgments

This book is dedicated to my parents, Mary and Pip Griffin, the initial source of magic and spirituality. They set me on this soul path from an early age and I am so forever grateful for this journey. Also to my family, my two children Holly and Harry Kenyon who are the ever-growing inspiration in my life.

A special shout out to my sisterhood for always encouraging me and having my back, who have helped me with this journey of creation and gave me inspiration and support. Also a thank you to all the women who appear in this book – thank you for allowing me to capture you.

Thank you to Coskewis for allowing me to be in your sacred land and to receive nature's wisdom and inspiration.

Thank you to my team at David and Charles who have brought my vision to life.

Lastly, to my husband Steve, who is my home, I couldn't do this without you. Thank you for all that you are.

Index

A DAVID AND CHARLES BOOK
© David and Charles, Ltd 2023

David and Charles is an imprint of
David and Charles, Ltd
Suite A, Tourism House, Pynes Hill,
Exeter, EX2 5WS

A catalogue record for this book is available from
the British Library.

ISBN-13: 9781446310021 paperback
ISBN-13: 9781446310090 EPUB
ISBN-13: 9781446310298 PDF

This book has been printed on paper from
approved suppliers and made from pulp from
sustainable sources.

Printed in China through Asia Pacific Offset for:
David and Charles, Ltd
Suite A, Tourism House, Pynes Hill,
Exeter, EX2 5WS

10 9 8 7 6 5 4 3 2 1

Publishing Director: Ame Verso
Senior Commissioning Editor: Lizzie Kaye
Managing Editor: Jeni Chown
Editor: Jessica Cropper
Project Editor: Clare Ashton
Head of Design: Anna Wade
Designer: Sam Staddon & Lee-May Lim
Pre-press Designer: Ali Stark
Illustrations: Emma Griffin
Photography & Art Direction: Emma Griffin
Production Manager: Beverley Richardson

David and Charles publishes high-quality
books on a wide range of subjects. For more
information visit **www.davidandcharles.com**.

Follow us on Instagram by searching for
@dandcbooks_wellbeing.

Layout of the digital edition of this book
may vary depending on reader hardware
and display settings.